AFROFUTURISM

AFROFUTURISM

THE WORLD OF BLACK SCI-FI AND FANTASY CULTURE

YTASHA L. WOMACK

Lawrence Hill Books

Chicago

Published by Lawrence Hill Books, an imprint of
Chicago Review Press, Incorporated
814 North Franklin Street
Chicago, Illinois 60610
ISBN 978-1-61374-796-4

Library of Congress Cataloging-in-Publication Data

Womack, Ytasha.
   Afrofuturism : the world of black sci-fi and fantasy culture / Ytasha L.
Womack. — First edition.
       pages cm
   Includes bibliographical references and index.
   ISBN 978-1-61374-796-4 (trade paper)
   1. Science fiction—Social aspects. 2. African Americans—Race identity.
3. Science fiction films—Influence. 4. Futurologists. 5. African diaspora—
Social conditions. I. Title.
   PN3433.5.W66 2013
   809.3'8762093529—dc23

                                      2013025755

Cover art and design: "Ioe Ostara" by John Jennings
Cover layout: Jonathan Hahn
Interior design: PerfecType, Nashville, TN
Interior art: John Jennings and James Marshall (p. 187)

Printed in the United States of America
10 9 8 7 6

I dedicate this book to Dr. Johnnie Colemon,
the first Afrofuturist to inspire my journey.
I dedicate this book to the legions of thinkers and futurists
who envision a loving world.

CONTENTS

ACKNOWLEDGMENTS

I would like to thank the stellar Lawrence Hill Books team: Cynthia Sherry, Michelle Schoob, Caitlin Eck, Mary Kravenas, and the many others who devoted their time and passion to bringing this book to light. Special thanks to John Jennings for his thoughtful insights and enlightening art. Thanks to John Jennings, Reynaldo Anderson, Shawn Wallace, and Stanford Carpenter for their willingness to throw mental softballs in the game of Afrofuturism mind chatter. I thank the many Afrofuturists, including Alondra Nelson and D. Denenge Akpem, who shared their work and ideas with me. I thank Linda and Leonard Murray, John Martin, Patrick Saingbey Woodtor, and Kerry James Marshall for their support. Thanks to curator Christine Mullen Kreamer for her heartfelt contributions. Thanks to Craig and Cory Stevenson for their artistic contributions. I thank my mom, Yvonne Womack, who willingly embarked on the Afrofuturism journey and gave me my first space suit. I thank my dad, Lloyd Womack, who unknowingly encouraged the cosplay imagination. I truly thank Susan Bradanini Betz, who believed in this project from the start and championed its existence.

INTRODUCTION

Who are you?" the Cheshire cat asked Alice in the mind-bending *Alice in Wonderland*. As a kid, I found the scary disappearing kooky kitten and his prickly questions nightmarish. When I got to the page where those glow-in-the-dark eyes in my Disney-friendly child-version storybook appeared, I'd flip the page faster than Gabby Douglas on the balance beam. Frightening, albeit intriguing. When Morpheus gives Neo the red pill/blue pill option, prefacing that he will find out just how deep the rabbit hole goes, *The Matrix* viewers know this is another tornado ride to Oz. No, Dorothy, you're not in Kansas anymore. And for those who adopt the Afrofuturist paradigm, the ideas can take you light-years away from the place you call home, only to return knowing you had had everything you needed from the start.

Readers, our future is now. Fortunately, there are guideposts on this worded journey through the cosmos, key archetypes that anchor the imagination on this spaceship ride dubbed "freedom": the Dogon's Sirius star, the fabled mermaid, the sky ark, a DJ scratch that blares like a Miles Davis horn, an ankh, a Yoruba deity, an Egyptian god, a body of water, a dancing robot, an Outkast ATLien. And there's electricity, lots of electricity,

1

nanotechnology, and plants. Someone may shout, "Wake up!" Others will echo chants of hope. Maybe you'll hop into a parallel universe with a past that reads like a fantasy or a future that feels like the past. But no trek is complete until you spot a sundial-sized headdress or that psychedelic wig. We like really big hair or no hair at all. Call it the power of the subconscious or the predominance of soul culture gone cyberpop, but this dance through time travel that Afrofuturists live for is as much about soul retrieval as it is about jettisoning into the far-off future, the uncharted Milky Way, or the depths of the subconscious and imagination.

Sun Ra, George Clinton, and Octavia Butler are sides of that Giza-like pyramid you find. Although the controls on the spaceship match your video game console, your life is not a video game. You are in cyberspace. Satellite maps don't work here. You cannot "check in," although you can click "like." No hyperlinks. If lost, get down to get up, go up to get down. If you must communicate, invent a communication device with a social media platform, and you'll be heard. Take photos, lots and lots of photos. Like every good hero, you have a digital soundtrack. But most important, you have nice reading material to smooth the ride. Oh, and you'll need sunglasses, really cool sunglasses.

Stay Spacetastic,
Ytasha

EVOLUTION

OF A SPACE CADET

1

When I was in the fourth grade, I was Princess Leia for Halloween. Leia, the princess and born leader of the rebel forces in *Star Wars Episode IV: A New Hope*, was my heroine in elementary school. It is a distinct memory, because wearing all white with a wooden sword on your hip in a rainstorm and trying to explain that you're a cosmic princess to candy-giving neighbors isn't a memory you forget. With two giant braids twisted into coils and pinned neatly on either side of my head, I found the idea of being a galactic princess with guts and brains to be pretty cool. Later, I would fully understand the myth of the Force and the archetypical battles between ego and light that render *Star Wars* fans so enthusiastic. But as a kid, I was a bit more infatuated with lightsabers and Ewoks and just glad that Luke and Leia didn't fall in love, because they were Jedi siblings.

While it was fun to be the chick from outer space in my imagination, the quest to see myself or browner people in this space age, galactic epic was important to me. Through the eyes of a child, the absence of such imagery didn't escape me. For one, I secretly wished that Lando Calrissian, played by sex symbol Billy Dee Williams, hadn't lost the *Millennium Falcon* in a bet—then maybe he, and not Han Solo, would have had more screen time navigating the solar systems. I wished that when Darth Vader's face was revealed, it would have been actor James Earl Jones, the real-life voice behind the mask, and not British thespian David Prowse who emerged. Then again, I also wished that Princess Leia and not Luke had been the first sibling trained in the way of the Jedi, and then I could have carried a lightsaber at Halloween instead of my brother's wooden sword.

While it would be easy to dismiss these wishes as childhood folly from yesteryear, it's in wishes like these—all a result of the obvious absence of people of color in the fictitious future/past (remember, it was a long time ago in a galaxy far, far away)—that seeds were planted in the imaginations of countless black kids who yearned to see themselves in warp-speed spaceships too. With the diversity of the nation and world increasingly standing in stark contrast to the diversity in futuristic works, it's no surprise that Afrofuturism emerged.

No surprise either that with Princess Leia a few solar returns behind me, I would create *Rayla 2212*, a multimedia series with music, books, animation, and games that follows Rayla Illmatic. Rayla is a rebel strategist and third-generation citizen of Planet Hope, an Earth colony gone rogue some two hundred years into the future. Her nickname is Princess, and she's charged with finding Moulan Shakur (note the Disney and Tupac shout-outs), a mysterious scientist who trains her to find the Missing. The journey takes her across worlds and lifetimes. And she's a browner woman. She's balancing her go-hard attitude with a penchant for love, she quotes twentieth- and twenty-first-century pop culture song lyrics like they're Shakespeare, and she wields a nice, shiny double-edged sword.

Friends and colleagues have joked that the 3-D animated image of Rayla reminds them of me.

No kidding.

Black to the Future

I was an Afrofuturist before the term existed. And any sci-fi fan, comic book geek, fantasy reader, Trekker, or science fair winner who ever wondered why black people are minimized in pop culture depictions of the future, conspicuously absent from the history of science, or marginalized in the roster of past inventors and then actually set out to do something about it could arguably qualify as an Afrofuturist as well.

It's one thing when black people aren't discussed in world history. Fortunately, teams of dedicated historians and culture advocates have chipped away at the propaganda often functioning as history for the world's students to eradicate that glaring error. But when, even in the imaginary future—a space where the mind can stretch beyond the Milky Way to envision routine space travel, cuddly space animals, talking apes, and time machines—people can't fathom a person of non-Euro descent a hundred years into the future, a cosmic foot has to be put down.

It was an age-old joke that blacks in sci-fi movies from the '50s through the '90s typically had a dour fate. The black man who saved the day in the original *Night of the Living Dead* was killed by trigger-happy cops. The black man who landed with Charlton Heston in the original *Planet of the Apes* was quickly captured and stuffed in a museum. An overeager black scientist nearly triggered the end of the world in *Terminator 2*. On occasion, the black character in such films popped up as the silent, mystical type or maybe a scary witch doctor, but it was fairly clear that in the artistic renderings of the future by pop culture standards, people of color weren't factors at all.

But then came the smash box-office success of *The Matrix* and *Avatar*. Both movies spoke to a reenvisioning of the future that weaved mysticism, explored the limits of technology, and advocated for self-expression and peace. *The Matrix* included a cast of multiethnic characters, the polar opposite of the legacy of homogeneous sci-fi depictions so great that even film critic Roger Ebert questioned whether *The Matrix* creators envisioned a future world dominated by black people. Then Denzel Washington played humanity's savior in the Hughes brothers' postapocalyptic film *The Book of Eli*. Wesley Snipes's heroic *Blade* trilogy inspired a new tier of black vampire heroes, not to mention a cosplay craze in which countless men donned the Blade costume.

Will Smith, summer blockbuster king and the consummate smart-talking good guy, was the sci-fi hero ushering in the new millennium. As an actor, he has saved Earth and greater humanity three times and counting, not including the time he outsmarted surveillance technology in *Enemy of the State*. Smith put a cosmic dent in the monolithic depiction of the sci-fi hero. He played a devoted scientist and last man on Earth working on a cure to save humanity from the zombie apocalypse in *I Am Legend*; he was the kick-butt war pilot who landed a mean hook on an alien and could fly galactic spacecraft, thus disabling the impending alien invasion in *Independence Day*; and he played a sunglasses-clad government agent devoted to keeping humans ignorant of the massive alien populations both friendly and hostile who frequent Earth in the *Men in Black* trilogy. In *After Earth*, Smith plays the father of a character played by his real-life son, Jaden Smith, on a distant planet some thousand years after Earth has been evacuated. Both men on a ride through space find themselves stranded on a very different Earth and the save-the-earth lineage continues. These cultural hallmarks aside, a larger culture of black sci-fi heads have now taken it upon themselves to create their own takes on futuristic life through the arts and critical theory. And the creations are groundbreaking.

What Is Afrofuturism?

Afrofuturism is an intersection of imagination, technology, the future, and liberation. "I generally define Afrofuturism as a way of imagining possible futures through a black cultural lens," says Ingrid LaFleur, an art curator and Afrofuturist. LaFleur presented for the independently organized TEDx Fort Greene Salon in Brooklyn, New York. "I see Afrofuturism as a way to encourage experimentation, reimagine identities, and activate liberation," she said.[1]

Whether through literature, visual arts, music, or grassroots organizing, Afrofuturists redefine culture and notions of blackness for today and the future. Both an artistic aesthetic and a framework for critical theory, Afrofuturism combines elements of science fiction, historical fiction, speculative fiction, fantasy, Afrocentricity, and magic realism with non-Western beliefs. In some cases, it's a total reenvisioning of the past and speculation about the future rife with cultural critiques.

Take William Hayashi's self-published novel *Discovery: Volume 1 of the Darkside Trilogy*. The story follows the discovery of rumored black American separatists whose disgust with racial disparity led them to create a society on the moon long before Neil Armstrong's arrival. The story is a commentary on separatist theory, race, and politics that inverts the nationalistic themes of the early space race.

Or take John Jennings and Stacey Robinson's *Black Kirby* exhibit, a touring tribute to legend Jack Kirby of Marvel and DC Comics fame. The show is a "What if Jack Kirby were black?" speculation depicting Kirby's iconic comic book covers using themes from black culture. The show displays parallels between black culture and Kirby's Jewish heritage, explores otherness and alienation, and adds new dimensions to the pop culture hero.

Afrofuturism can weave mysticism with its social commentary too. Award-winning fiction writer Nnedi Okorafor's *Who Fears Death* captures the struggles of Onyesonwu, a woman in post-nuclear, apocalyptic Africa who is under the tutelage of a shaman. She hopes to use her newfound gifts to save her people from genocide.

Whether it's the African futuristic fashion of former Diddy-Dirty Money songstress Dawn Richard—which she unveiled in her music videos for the digital album *Goldenheart*—or the indie film and video game *Project Fly*, which was created by DJ James Quake and follows a group of black ninjas on Chicago's South Side, the creativity born from rooting black culture in sci-fi and fantasy is an exciting evolution.

This blossoming culture is unique. Unlike previous eras, today's artists can wield the power of digital media, social platforms, digital video, graphic arts, gaming technology, and more to tell their stories, share their stories, and connect with audiences inexpensively—a gift from the sci-fi gods, so to speak, that was unthinkable at the turn of the century. The storytelling gatekeepers vanished with the high-speed modem, and for the first time in history, people of color have a greater ability to project their own stories. This tug-and-pull debate over black people controlling their image shifts considerably when a fledgling filmmaker can shoot his sci-fi web series on a $500 DV cam, post it on YouTube, and promote it on Instagram and Twitter.

While technology empowers creators, this intrigue with sci-fi and fantasy itself inverts conventional thinking about black identity and holds the imagination supreme. Black identity does not have to be a negotiation with awful stereotypes, a dystopian view of the race (remember those black-man-as-endangered-species stories or the constant "Why are black women single?" reports?), an abysmal sense of powerlessness, or a reckoning of hardened realities. Fatalism is not a synonym for blackness.

If a story line or an artist's disposition wasn't washed in fatalism, southern edicts, or urbanized reality, then some questioned whether it was even "black." Sci-fi vanguard and writer Octavia Butler, who authored the famous *Parable* series and laid the groundwork for countless sci-fi heroines and writers to follow, said it never failed that she'd be confronted by someone at a conference who would ask, "Just what does science fiction have to do with black people?"

Rise of the Black Geek

More than just a hipster fashion statement where big glasses, tight suits, and high-water pants are the norm, the black geek phenomenon normalizes all things formally couched as geeky. Science lovers, space dreamers, comic book fans, techies, or anyone who relishes super-high-level analysis just for the fun of it could be a geek, according to conventional wisdom. Today, such interests are cool, functional, and often necessary—or at least there's a larger world where those of like minds can find one another online and aren't limited to hanging out with, say, the one other kid on the block who likes quantum physics. A decade or two ago, many kids had to hide their love affairs in a swathe of coolness, athleticism, and popularity or face being isolated and teased to no end. Documentarian Tony Williams's latest project, *Carbonerdious: Rise of the Black Nerd*, chronicles this shift in geekness. A self-described techie and music and comic lover, he admits to being a geek and has scoured the country interviewing black geeks from all walks of life. In fact, the finesse of geekdom was celebrated at the University of Illinois's 2013 Black Geek Week, a week of panels featuring scientists, animators, comic book illustrators, science fiction writers, and technology experts, most of whom grew up in families that encouraged a strong cultural identity and natural curiosity that rooted them in ways that made the panelists comfortable being left of center. I participated as well, and I was struck by the sense of duty accompanying the panelists. Today, these closeted and not-so-closeted geeks embraced this once-feared word like a badge of honor, the ultimate reward for their persistence, intelligence, wit, and the pure hell they often withstood when sharing their geekdom with unappreciative peers. Today, those geeks are on the upswing, working in the tech industry, owning comic book stores, illustrating as animators, or studying in labs across the country. All those lonely hours of work, those hellacious awkward years, and the moments of isolation have paid off.

In fact, when I shared in passing with a few people, fresh off the conference trail, that I attended a black geek affair, the listeners confided that they, despite their suits or swag, were really geeks, too. But this bonding moment had happened before. The notion surfaced at author Baratunde Thurston's *How to Be Black* book release party, where after hearing several satirical but true tales, people confided about their geek past to one another. Stories were shared at a Vocalo.org storytelling hour, where participants shared tales of growing comfortable with their inner geek. People all over the country were revealing the giant Gs on their chests: part confession, part pride, all with a longing to have honor restored. Had the inner geek become a bonding mechanism? Although the black geek isn't new to America's shores—black America has a history of black geeks and intellectuals, although being a geek and an intellectual isn't always the same thing—the celebration totally shatters limited notions of black identity. Mia Coleman, a die-hard science fiction fan who travels the country to attend sci-fi conventions, sometimes applying for support from the Carl Brandon Society, an organization designed to encourage diversity in sci-fi, says that the genre is the perfect space for those who don't fit in. "I love science fiction; it can save people's lives. If you feel weird, there's a big place that will embrace you. Instead of feeling weird and isolated, it brings people together."

Cosplay Rules

The same goes for cosplay. Cosplay, or the act of donning costumes from your favorite comic book, video game, manga, or anime tale, is pretty popular, totally geeky, and truly fun. There's a large number of black participants in the cosplay community, each dressed as his or her favorite hero or heroine at the ComicCons and other cosplay parties across the country. From Storm to Blade, Batman to Supergirl, Green Lantern to Black Panther, black cosplay fans adopt the mannerisms, costumes, and makeup of them all. At the last ComicCon I attended, I spotted a man dressed as Django, the vigilante former slave in the film *Django Unchained*. A friend of mine spotted a father-daughter Martian team.

This open play with the imagination, one that isn't limited to Halloween or film, is a break from identity, one that mirrors the dress-up antics associated with George Clinton, Grace Jones, and other eccentric luminaries now dubbed Afrofuturists. While it's all play, there's a power in breaking past rigid identity parameters and adopting the persona of one's favorite hero.

"Cosplay is a form of empowerment for all children and adults," says Stanford Carpenter, president and cofounder of the Institute for Comics Studies, who says that he used to be dismissive of cosplay. But after attending dozens of ComicCons, he witnessed the dress-up affair changing masked heroes indefinitely. "It's about empowerment. It's about the possibility of what you can be or what you can do. And when you see people in underrepresented groups, it takes on the empowerment fantasy of not just, say, being Superman, but also the dimension of stepping on the much more narrow roles that we are assigned. But this idea of this superhero has an added dimension because it inherently pushes against many of the stereotypes that are thrust upon us. It is this opportunity to push the boundaries of what you can be and in so doing, you're imagining a whole new world and possibilities for yourself that can extend beyond the cosplay experience," says Carpenter. "It's like stepping to the top of the mountaintop where everything looks small. It's not that you stay on the mountain top forever, but when you come down you're not the same. You have a new perspective. A choice that you don't know is a choice that you don't have. The imagination is the greatest resource that humans have. Cosplay builds on that. Cosplay puts imagination and desire into action in a way that allows people to look at things differently."

What do black geek conferences, geek confessions, space warrior princesses, and excitable black fans dressed like Green Lantern and Blade have to do with progress? Everything.

Afrofuturism unchains the mind. This charge to spur critical thinking is why museums including the Tubman African-American Museum in Macon, Georgia, the Sargent Johnson Gallery in Oakland, and the Museum of Contemporary Diasporan Arts in Brooklyn championed Afrofuturism exhibits, all hoping to engage children and nontraditional art communities.

"It gives our young people another out," says Melorra Green, visual arts coordinator of the Sargent Johnson Gallery in Oakland. "They need to see people stepping outside of the norm."

I remember a twenty-something African American woman who took my screenwriting class once. She was incredibly frustrated because she wanted to write a historical fiction narrative with black characters but felt thwarted by the realities of racism in the past. There could be no cowboy hero, no Victorian romance, no antebellum South epic, or any other story without the cloud of slavery or colonialism to doom her character's fate. She couldn't come up with a single story idea that could have a happy ending, at least not one that took place in the past five hundred years, up to, say, 1960. As for writing sci-fi or creating a world in the future or coming up with a complete fantasy, she didn't know how she could integrate black culture into the story. The parameters of race had completely chained her imagination.

One movement that counteracts historical assumptions is the steampunk movement, which has a large black subculture. In fact, the books and illustrations emerging from the culture are deemed steamfunk. Steampunk is a sci-fi subgenre that uses steam-powered technology from the eras of the old West and Victorian age as the backdrop for alternative-history sagas. The stories are as lively as the real-world steampunk fashionistas, a legion of nineteenth-century-fixated, corset-wearing petticoat lovers who modernize the top hat and pocket watch for the current era.

At its heart, Afrofuturism stretches the imagination far beyond the conventions of our time and the horizons of expectation, and kicks the box of normalcy and preconceived ideas of blackness out of the solar system. Whether it's sci-fi story lines or radical eccentricity, Afrofuturism inverts reality.

Afrofuturists write their own stories.

"Afrofuturism, like post blackness, destabilizes previous analysis of blackness," says Reynaldo Anderson, assistant professor of humanities at Harris-Stowe State University and a writer of Afrofuturist critical theory. "What I like about Afrofuturism is it helps create our own space in the future; it allows us to control our imagination," he says. "An Afrofuturist is not ignorant of history, but they don't let history restrain their creative impulses either."

The Dawn of a New Era

Afrofuturism as a term was coined by cultural critic Mark Dery, who used it in his 1994 essay "Black to the Future" to describe a flurry of analysis fueled by sci-fi-loving black college students and artists who were passionately reframing discussions about art and social change through the lens of science and technology in the 1980s and '90s. Dery ushered in the serious study of cyberculture and gave a name to the technoculture trends in black America. Music and culture writers Greg Tate, Mark Sinker, and Kodwo Eshun were among the earliest Afrofuturism theorists, paralleling Dery's interest. The roots of the aesthetic began decades before, but with the emergence of Afrofuturism as a philosophical study, suddenly artists like avant-garde jazz legend Sun Ra, funk pioneer George Clinton, and sci-fi author Octavia Butler were rediscovered and reframed by Afrofuturists as social change agents.

The role of science and technology in the black experience overall was unearthed and viewed from new perspectives. Black musical innovators were being studied for their use and creation of progressive technologies. Inventors like Joseph Hunter Dickinson, who made innovations to the player piano and record player, were viewed as champions in black musical production. Jimi Hendrix's use of reverb on his guitar was reframed as a part of a black musical and scientific legacy. Others explored the historical social impact of technological advances on people of African descent and how they were wielded to affirm racial divisions or to overcome them.

And many found the parallels between sci-fi themes of alien abduction and the transatlantic slave trade to be both haunting and fascinating. Were stories about aliens really just metaphors for the experience of blacks in the Americas?

Afrofuturists sought to unearth the missing history of people of African descent and their roles in science, technology, and science fiction. They also aimed to reintegrate people of color into the discussion of cyberculture, modern science, technology, and sci-fi pop culture. With the Internet in its infancy, they hoped to facilitate equal access to progressive technologies, knowing that a widespread embrace would diminish the race-based power imbalance—and hopefully color-based limitations—for good.

A Cyber Movement Is Born

Graduate student Alondra Nelson was living in New York City in the late 1990s when she launched an AOL Listserv, an early Internet discussion pool, for students and artists who wanted to explore ideas about technology, space, freedom, culture, and art with science fiction as the centrifuge. Nelson was a sci-fi fan and saw parallels between popular themes in science fiction and themes in the history and culture of people of African descent in the Americas. She especially resonated with the theme of cultural abduction and with the unsung black scientists who were often missing from history books.

"The first moderator was DJ Spooky," Nelson says, referring to the DJ well known for remixing the film *The Birth of a Nation* live in a touring set. Others, including award-winning sci-fi author Nalo Hopkinson and theorist Alexander Weheliye, signed on too. "It became a rich site for sharing," Nelson says. The site became a Yahoo! group, and then a Google group, and eventually someone put up a website. By 2000, Nelson was writing on Afrofuturism for *Colorlines.* "I wrote about the community and what we were trying to do," she says.

Discussions of art, human rights, or cultural hallmarks among people of African descent in this vein were new and exciting. There existed a host of writings and creations that were a bit left of the cultural paradigm and hadn't previously fit neatly into any existing arts movements, and this new space-tinged prism gave them a context.

As more long-lost works were uncovered and discussed in this new framework, it became clear that there was a tradition of sci-fi or futuristic works created by people of African descent that stretched back to precolonial Africa. More recently, being imaginative and creative, and even projecting black culture into the future, was part of a lineage of resistance to daunting power structures. The conversations around these subjects led others to create new works and find old ones, and an enthusiasm to document the movement ensued. Suddenly the world of black sci-fi geeks and comic book fans who felt isolated in their interests and ignored by mainstream sci-fi creators had a virtual home, an aesthetic to give their craft and pastime an academically based validity.

The idea of Afrofuturism was groundbreaking, as was the use of the blossoming Internet space that facilitated the conversation. "It would have been much more difficult to have the conversation ten years earlier," says Alexander Weheliye, now a professor who teaches Afrofuturism and postintegration perspectives at Northwestern University.

Many of the leading Afrofuturism professors and artists were participants on the Listserv. "Being on the Listserv provided a space for our ideas," Weheliye says. Nelson pushed the conversation of Afrofuturism beyond artistic analysis to the point of creating change for the future.

The name Afrofuturism itself toiled largely in academic and arts circles, specifically those circles that were engaged in the conversation. Even today many people creating Afrofuturistic work are newcomers to the term. But the idea of creating more works with people of color in sci-fi and exploring the idea of blacks in the future is spreading like wildfire.

The Internet continues to be the primary gathering site for Afrofuturists. In 2008 Jarvis Sheffield created BlackScience Fiction.com, a website for sci-fi artists, writers, filmmakers, and animators. Riding high off the election of President Barack Obama, Sheffield, a comic book fan and a father, wanted to create a site with diverse images for his son. The site launched with ten profiles. In 2012 it had 2,016. "I'm addicted to the site. Every week someone posts something new," says Sheffield. He assembled works from featured writers on the website and released *Genesis: An Anthology of Black Science Fiction* in two volumes. Today, the site is a major portal for sci-fi creators.

The Mothership Lands on a Historically Black College and University (HBCU)

My introduction to what I would later learn was Afrofuturism began in college. I didn't know Nelson. I didn't know Dery. But I did know crews of campus students in the Clark Atlanta, Morehouse, Spelman, and Morris Brown quads who would gather between and after classes to converse. They were honor bound to the links between black history and science fiction, and rooted in the belief that more art and critical theory on the subject could spawn social change.

Since these college crews were on an upwardly mobile path to enlightenment just years shy of the dawn of the twenty-first century, you could find yourself debating everything from the metaphors in the latest underground hip-hop release to the validity of the Book of Genesis. It was nothing formal, maybe a meeting of two minds, nothing more. But the logic in the cyclical equations this cadre of urban philosophers shared zigzagged from quantum physics to African philosophy to film aesthetics to economic theories to music theory and back. The reasoning always put people of color square at the heart of the theorem. The plight of black people collectively lined the hypothesis, formulated the body and the conclusion, and somehow always tied into a future and past as intricately woven as strands of DNA.

Kamafi, a Philly-born honors history and physics major, launched an underground newspaper on the subject that posted essays and art from fellow students. Outspoken, smart as a whip, and proud, he embodied the hip-hop aesthetic like a warrior's cloak and was a self-proclaimed "Du Boisian" who got a kick out of destroying people's ivory towers with earth-rooted knowledge. I like to think I was one of the few who weren't thrown for a loop with his mojo bag of theories, but he did throw at least one at me that had me dazzled: his breakdown on Parliament/Funkadelic.

At the time, I didn't see the depth of "One Nation Under a Groove" or "Freak of the Week" beyond their mesmerizing bass lines. He proceeded to explain the Parliament/Funkadelic cosmology—a winding galactic tale in which funk doubled as the Force à la *Star Wars* in a space-age tale that poised wrongdoers against light-seekers, all told in a series of albums. He echoed the double entendres in the work, the multiple layers in various lyrics. And just when I was about to argue that he was making the whole thing up, I realized that he was on to something.

Because the aesthetic in the music was popping up in hip-hop and neo-soul lyrics. Songstress Erykah Badu, who minored in physics while attending Grambling University, another HBCU, made casual references to the P-Funk mothership and quantum physics. As a newfound resident Atlantan, I was under the spell of Outkast's second album, deftly titled *ATLiens*. Between the streams of college kids who wanted to debate *Star Wars* and the unearthing of P-Funk in '90s-era hip-hop, the brewing of an aesthetic was obvious. A budding culture of artists and sci-fi fans was using art and media platforms to explore humanity and the experiences of people in the African diaspora in futuristic works.

Over the years, I became fascinated by the growing number of artists I encountered who were developing art exploring people of color and the future. Visual artists, graphic artists, musicians, poets, DJs, dancers, writers, and filmmakers—each immersed in works with strong sci-fi and historical fiction themes, often flirting with an Eastern or African philosophy, and all utilizing black characters or aesthetics to deconstruct images of the past to revisualize the future.

I went to the Museum of Contemporary Art in Chicago to see DJ Spooky's revisualization of the film *The Birth of a Nation*, with live DJ scratches and break beats underscoring a reedited, rhythmic version of the characters in blackface. I met artists like Nicole Mitchell, a jazz flutist and composer who wrote a composition in honor of Octavia Butler, and Chris Adams and Jonathan Woods, video directors who incorporated sci-fi images and themes in their work. Increasingly, I found myself meeting artists who were digging to create a digital future with a pensive urgency only matched by a growing culture of African Americans flipping through films and comic books, music and novels, seeking those very creations.

It was all food for thought in a growing mental list for my own private study. Clearly this line of research was uncategorizable—some good-natured pop psychology that bound fiction and fantasy with historical elements thrown in to lend weight to long-winding debates. Then one day I was in Chicago at an art show at the G. R. N'Namdi Gallery. The gallery was bubbling with springtime collectors and artists, elated that the weather was finally warming, when I met a woman whose offhand commentary piqued my curiosity. D. Denenge Akpem, an artist and professor I'd met once before, mentioned that she was teaching a new class at Columbia College in Chicago. "I'm teaching Afrofuturism," she remarked. Immediately my mind warp-sped to my college years and the cult of analysis among classmates who discussed cultural phenomena. While I'd never heard the term Afrofuturism before, I knew exactly what she was talking about. "You mean, they're teaching this in schools now?" I asked. Her response was, "Well, yes."

After the shock wore off, I figured, Why wouldn't they?

There's a burgeoning group of professors, much like the famed hip-hop professors who emerged a decade ago, who are dedicated to the study of works that analyze dynamics of race and culture specific to the experiences of black people through sci-fi and fantasy works. They use it as a platform to assess humanity issues—including war, apartheid, and genocide—while also exploring class issues, spirituality, philosophy, and history. Others reevaluate the use of technology, its use in society, and its role in the creation of art as a process. Still others look to these analyses as methodologies to free people from mental blocks and societal limitations. But each, from the artist to the professor to the fan, prioritizes the reenvisioning of people of color in a shared harmonious future free of race-based power issues. At the very least, they create a future with people of color integrally involved—a demonstration that counters pop culture's relative failure to do so.

It's fitting that this book is being published after the reelection of the nation's first African American president. A dream held dear by the futurists of the past, not so long ago the rise of the president would have been in the realms of science fiction. Today, the future is now. The first human voice broadcast from Mars was that of NASA director Charles F. Bolden, a Houston-born retired marine and former astronaut who is also African American. The president has charged NASA to land on an asteroid by 2025, and private enterprise Mars One is taking applications for Earthlings to launch a Mars colony by 2023. We are at the dawn of the commercial space era. The intersection of imagination, technology, culture, and innovation is pivotal. The synergy of the four creates an informed prism that can redefine lifestyles, worldviews, and beliefs. Afrofuturism is often the umbrella for an amalgamation of narratives, but at the core, it values the power of creativity and imagination to reinvigorate culture and transcend social limitations. The resilience of the human spirit lies in our ability to imagine.

The imagination is a tool of resistance. Creating stories with people of color in the future defies the norm. With the power of technology and emerging freedoms, black artists have more control over their image than ever before.

Welcome to the future.

When I was in college, I remember my African American History teacher posing a question that would forever change our lives. "Which came first," she asked, "racism or slavery?" My classmates, all of whom considered themselves to be quasi black history experts, were firm in their answer: racism. We believed that those who led the transatlantic slave trade and infused laws to support it had an intrinsic belief that people of darker skin were inferior and thus they enslaved them. But we were wrong. Slavery, she said, came first, and racism was created to justify it. We argued with her, because for us, it simply didn't make any sense. Race, we believed, always existed. But race, we soon realized, despite our pride, was a creation too.

Soon after I wrote *Post Black*, race as a political creation that we'd all come to live with as this fixed division became so obvious that I began including it in my book chats as part of my official stump speech. When I met artist and filmmaker Cauleen Smith in July 2011, she best summed up race as creation: "Blackness is a technology," said Smith. "It's not real. It's a thing."

Dorothy Roberts, Northwestern University professor and medical-ethics advocate, calls race "the fatal invention." She writes extensively about medical and health experts falsely using race and DNA to make medical determinations.

"I decided to write [the book *Fatal Invention*] because I have noticed resurgence in the use of the term race as a biological category. And also [I noticed] a growing acceptance among colleagues and speakers that race really is biological and somehow genomic science will soon discover the biological truths about race," says Roberts. "The more I looked into it, I saw there were more scientists that said they discovered race in the genes, and more products coming out showing that race is a natural division."[1]

Race as a biological entity has seeped into conventional wisdom with both blacks and whites at various times, using the invention to explain power imbalances and superiority. Even Nation of Islam founder Elijah Muhammad taught that the white race was invented by an evil scientist. Others, in an attempt to counter racism, developed an odd science claiming that melanin gave brown people better intuitive or superhuman abilities.

Frankly, as much as people analyze race in the public discourse, it's rarely discussed as an invention to regulate social order. Even those who advocate against injustice rarely broach race as a creation. The argument could have the same consequences as that of post-racialists, who say that racial divisions no longer exist. How does one discuss the realities of the pain and social maladies caused by lack of equity and at the same time say that race is a creation? Are the injustices imagined too? When Roberts was a guest, and I a guest cohost, on WVON's *Matt McGill Morning Show* in Chicago, one angered caller asked, "Well, if race is an invention and not real, how do you explain racism?" Roberts shared that the politics and social measures as well as the laws and injustices around race are real. However, race is not some default biological category, although it is a social and political identity.

The whole contemplation ripped the lid off a Pandora's box of questions for me. What decisions do we make because of the limitations or expectations we associate with race? If we cast off those limitations, how would our social lives change? Would we have the same friendships? Live in the same neighborhoods? Go to the same schools? I'd pose these questions to audiences, and it was a daunting thought. Outer obstacles aside, what role have we played in limiting our own lives based on race? This contemplation ultimately led to the *Rayla 2212* series. I wanted to write about a world of people of color where race as we know it today was not a factor. But I also wanted the challenge of writing about people of color without using today's ethnic cultures as an identity or backdrop while still denoting the value of the cultures in their past and our present. It was a very Afrofuturistic experiment. For that, I had to take my story to space.

The Birth of the Post-Human

In the fall of 2011, I received a call from Hank Pellissier, then a fellow with the Institute for Ethics and Emerging Technologies. Pellissier was looking for futurists to submit essays. The institute is also a proponent of transhumanism, a futurist philosophy that explores the possibilities of a post-human life. Being human, as we understand it today, could evolve with new technologies. Could science extend our life span by three hundred years? Could new medicine curtail the need for sleep? Transhumanists believe in maximizing human potential and look to exceed human limitations, physical and otherwise, with new medicine, nanotechnology, or robotic culture. Some transhumanists boldly claim that by 2045, humans will officially merge with machines. Ironic, I thought, because that same decade is predicted to mark the beginning of the majority-minority America.

Nevertheless, transhumanism is a fascinating concept. One day being plain old human could be old school. Physicalities like childbirth (which is already being revolutionized), eating, or death could be tokens of the distant past. But in stretching my imagination to grasp the prospects of post-human life, I found myself thinking about what it means to be human.

We don't give a great deal of thought to being human, although history is marred with theories about and battles over human rights. While some politics and rights are debated, there are some agreed-upon human rights that supersede nationality, politics, and expectations—human rights that are deemed inalienable. Life, liberty, and the security of person are among those espoused in the UN's Universal Declaration of Human Rights, as well as the belief that we're all "born free."

At least this is the general consensus today.

But at one point in history, just as monarchies challenged Galileo on his Earth-revolving-around-the-sun theory, scientists and profiteers argued about just who was human and who was not. A color-based, sex-based hierarchy was formed largely to regulate who had access to the world's resources and rights of self-determination and who did not.

The concept is a weird one. One of the most difficult ideas for descendants of enslaved Africans to swallow is that at one point in time, our ancestors were not deemed human. This wasn't just an opinion, but rather a legal status encoded in the first version of the US Constitution. By law, enslaved Africans were three-fifths human. None of the rights to life, liberty, and the pursuit of happiness that we so proudly celebrate today were extended to women, Native Americans, or anyone who was not a white male. Citizenship rights were only granted to those who were legally human.

"Black people in America came here as chattel, so we've had to constantly prove our humanity," says San Francisco poet and Afro-surrealist D. Scot Miller. "I'm not a shovel, I'm not a horse, I'm a full-blown human being. It's absurd."

In Steven Spielberg's film *Lincoln*, there's a pivotal scene in which radical Republican and antislavery advocate Thaddeus Stephens is drilled by his fellow Congressmen on whether blacks and whites are equal under God or just equal under the law. To convince pro-slavery lawmakers to pass the Thirteenth Amendment abolishing slavery, Stephens had to go against his own code of ethics and emphasize that the soon-to-be-freed slaves should be equal under the law and no more. Watching this dramatic negotiation of human status by lawmakers was heart-wrenching.

Now, the Constitution prior to the Thirteenth Amendment didn't decree that blacks were aliens, or at least it didn't use those words. Those who profited from westward expansion didn't quite say that people of African descent were rocketed from a distant star, either. However, those invested in this new color-based power imbalance did push literature and fake science deeming people of African descent and browner peoples in general as hovering on the lower end of the Darwinian scale. No, they didn't hail from a planet in another solar system, but they were from another world, with mysterious lands and customs that were devalued and vilified to dehumanize.

This dehumanization was wrongfully encoded in laws, violently enforced, perpetuated by propaganda and stereotypes, and falsely substantiated by inaccurate science, all to justify a swath of violent atrocities in the name of greed. Humans have used these methods to dehumanize others. The transatlantic slave trade, Jim Crow in the American South, South African apartheid, the Holocaust in Europe, ethnic cleansing in the former Yugoslavia and in Rwanda, and the massacre of native peoples throughout the world were waged on the basis of others being nonhuman.

What Does It Mean to Be Human?

British writer Mark Sinker was arguably the first to ask, "What does it mean to be human?" in what would later be called the Afrofuturistic context. Sinker, then a writer for *Wired*, posed the question and explored the aspirations, sci-fi themes, and technology in jazz, funk, and hip-hop music.

"In other words, Mark made the correlation between *Blade Runner* and slavery, between the idea of alien abduction and the real events of slavery," writes Kodwo Eshun. "It was an amazing thing, because as soon as I read this, I thought, my God, it just allows so many things."[2]

Dery identified the parallels in "Black to the Future" as well. "African Americans are, in a very real sense, the descendants of alien abductees," Dery writes. He compares the atrocities of racism experienced by blacks in the United States to "a sci-fi nightmare in which unseen but no less impassable force fields of intolerance frustrate their movement; official histories undo what has been done; and technology is too often brought to bear on black bodies (branding, forced sterilization, the Tuskegee experiment, and tasers come readily to mind)."[3]

Dery and Sinker were not the first to explore the deplorable need of some to dehumanize others in the quest for power. Yet their frameworks led to Afrofuturistic writings that for the first time linked the transatlantic slave trade to a metaphor of alien abduction.

What does it mean to be nonhuman? As a nonhuman, your life is not valued. You are an "alien," "foreign," "exotic," "savage"— a wild one to be conquered or a nuisance to be destroyed. Your bodies are not your own, fit for probing and research. You have no history of value. You are incapable of creating culture in general, but when you do, it is from an impulse or emotion, never intellect. Humans, well meaning or otherwise, can't relate to a nonhuman.

Even the term "illegal alien," often used for undocumented workers moving to nations across the world, plays off fears of otherness, invasion, and takeover. The fear fanned by the fast-approaching minority-majority nation shift in the United States has led to hotly debated laws and policies that mostly target Latino immigrants. Advocates charge that racial profiling and other human-rights violations are on the upswing as undocumented workers and those who fit the ethnic description of the stereotyped "illegal alien" fall prey to unjust attacks, violence, or surveillance.

The greater part of the civil rights movement in the United States, as well as self-rule movements in precolonial India, the Caribbean, and on the African continent, were efforts to ensure equal rights for all. And this struggle paralleled equal efforts to prove that people of color, women, LGBTQ people, the working class, and others were in fact human.

The burden of having to prove one's humanity has defined the attainment of some of the greatest human rights achievements of our times as well as some of the greatest artistic works.

However, this notion of otherness prevails.

The Other Side of the Rainbow

The alien metaphor is one of the most common tropes in science fiction. Whether they are invading, as in *Independence Day*; the ultimate enemy, as portrayed in *Alien*; or misunderstood, like in *E.T.*, there is a societal lesson of conquering or tolerance that reminds viewers of real-life human divisions.

Other films are more explicit in the racial metaphor. *District 9*, a film set in South Africa about segregated alien settlements, was inspired by the horrors of Cape Town's District Six during the apartheid era. *Avatar* is a thinly veiled commentary on imperialism and indigenous cultures. And *The Brother from Another Planet* depicts an extraterrestrial in the form of a black man confused by the racial norms of the day.

Much of the science fiction fascination with earthbound alien encounters is preoccupied with how both cultures could merge and the turmoil that would ensue from overcoming perceptions of difference.

But other artists have compared their wrestling with W. E. B. Du Bois's double consciousness or the struggle of being both American and black with alien motifs. Artists from Sun Ra to Lil Wayne have referenced being alien to explain isolation.

Author Saidiya Hartman wrote in her book *Lose Your Mother* about feeling trapped in a racial paradox: "Was it why I sometimes felt as weary of America as if I too had landed in what was now South Carolina in 1526 or in Jamestown in 1619? Was it the tug of all the lost mothers and orphaned children? Or was it that each generation felt anew the yoke of a damaged life and the distress of being a native stranger, an eternal alien?"[4]

Theorists and the Double Alien

"I think that using alien to describe otherness works," says Reynaldo Anderson, a professor who writes about Afrofuturism. Anderson is one of many theorists who view the alien metaphor as one that explains the looming space of otherness perpetuated by the idea of race. "We're among the first alien abductees, kidnapped by strange people who take us over by ships and conduct scientific experiments on us. They bred us. They came up with a taxonomy of the people they bred: mulatto, octoroon, quadroon."

He adds that the scientific experimentations conducted in the name of race mimic sci-fi horror flicks. Henrietta Lacks was a 1950s Virginia tobacco farmer whose cells were taken without her permission and used to create immortal cell lines sold for research around the world. Named HeLa, these cell lines lived past Lacks's own death and were essential to the development of the polio vaccine, cloning, gene mapping, and in vitro fertilization. They were even sent in the first space missions to see what would happen to cells in zero gravity.

The alien concept has been expanded to explain isolation as well, with studies of "the black geek" in literature and an array of self-created modalities that infer a discomfort in one's own skin. In summer 2012, Emory University's African-American Studies Collective issued a call for papers for their 2013 conference, titled "Alien Bodies: Race, Space, and Sex in the African Diaspora." Held February 8 and 9, 2013, the conference examined the alien-as-race idea and looked at transformative tools to empower those who are alienated. It explored how "we begin to understand the ways in which race, space and sex configure 'the alien' within spaces allegedly 'beyond' markers of difference" and asked, "What are some ways in which the 'alien from within as well as without' can be overcome, and how do we make them sustainable?"

Afrofuturist academics are looking at alien motifs as a progressive framework to examine how those who are alienated adopt modes of resistance and transformation.

Stranger Than Science Fiction

Truth is stranger than fiction, but is truth stranger than science fiction too? Talk about real-time: science fiction has introduced a flash of technologies that our world is catching up to—the Internet, commercial space flights, smartphones, and the discovery of the Higgs boson, or "God Particle"—to name a few. In some ways we've surpassed the sci-fi canon.

Afrofuturism is concerned with both the impact of these technologies on social conditions and with the power of such technologies to end the "-isms" for good and safeguard humanity. Historically, new technologies have emerged with a double-edged sword, deepening as many divides as they build social bridges. Gunpowder was a technology that empowered colonizers and gave them the undeniable edge in creating color-based caste systems. Early forays into genetics were created to link ethnic physical traits with intelligence, thus falsely justifying dehumanization, slavery, and holocausts across the globe.

The Tuskegee experiment, in which innocent black men were injected with syphilis for scientific study, or the use of the immortal cells of Henrietta Lacks are evidence of how profit and the race to discovery must be tempered with strong ethics. "HeLa cells were the first human biological materials ever bought and sold, which helped launch a multibillion-dollar industry," says Rebecca Skloot, author of a book on Lack's immortal cells. "When [Lack's family] found out that people were selling vials of their mother's cells, and that the family didn't get any of the resulting money, they got very angry."[4]

Dorothy Roberts writes about how race is inappropriately used in medical research and to market products. "There are studies to explain racial divisions in health that are actually caused by social inequalities," Roberts said in her interview with me for my blog *The Post Black Experience* (http://postblackexperience .com). She continued, "Yet you have researchers studying high blood pressure, asthma among blacks, etc., and looking for a genetic cause. However, research shows these [illnesses] are the effects of racial inequality and the stress of racial inequality."[5] Although ethics and emerging technologies is a discussion that all futurists are concerned with, Afrofuturists, in particular, are highly sensitive to how or if such technologies will deepen or transcend the imbalances of race.

Son of Saturn

The alien motif reveals dissonance while also providing a prism through which to view the power of the imagination, aspiration, and creativity channeled in resisting dehumanization efforts. "The most important thing about Afrofuturism is to know that there have always been alternatives in what has been given in the present," says Alexander Weheliye. "I am not making light of the history of enslavement and medical experimentation," he continues, "but black people have always developed alternate ways of existing outside of these oppressions."

Improvisation, adaptability, and imagination are the core components of this resistance and are evident both in the arts and black cultures at large. Jazz, hip-hop, and blues are artistic examples, but there are ways of life that are based on improvisation, too, that aren't fully understood. "Of all the thousands of tribes on the continent, what they all share is this respect for improvisation," says Smith. "That idea in and of itself is a form of technology. In the Western world, improvisation is a failure; you do it when something goes wrong. But when black people improvise it's a form of mastery."

In Reynaldo Anderson's essay "Cultural Studies or Critical Afrofuturism: A Case Study in Visual Rhetoric, Sequential Art, and Post-Apocalyptic Black Identity," he talks about the notion of twinness as a form of resistance that pulled on Africanisms but also was uniquely formulated for survival. This survival took place in postapocalyptic times, with the transatlantic slave trade being the apocalypse, he says. Noting that African slaves came from societies in which women and men had equal governing power, Anderson says that "to be a human being an individual should possess both masculine and feminine principles (protector-nurturer) in order to have a healthy community." This twinness, he adds, was a survival mechanism "that enabled [women] to psychologically shield themselves and their inner lives." However, he also says that rhetorical strategies include signifying, call-and-response, narrative sequencing, tonal semantics, technological rhetoric, agitation, nationalism, jeremiads, nommo, Africana womanist or black feminist epistemologies, queer studies, time and space, visual rhetoric, and culture as modes of resistance.[6] But the point of this alien and postapocalyptic metaphor, says Anderson, isn't to get lost in traumas of the past or present-day alienation. The alien framework is a framework for understanding and healing.

It's the reason that D. Denenge Akpem teaches an Afrofuturism class as a pathway to liberation. "The basic premise of this course is that the creative ability to manifest action and transformation has been essential to the survival of Blacks in the Diaspora," she says.

The liberation edict in Afrofuturism provides a prism for evolution.

3

PROJECT
IMAGINATION

an you imagine a world without the idea of race? Can you imagine a world where skin color, hair texture, national origin, and ethnicity are not determinants of power, class, beauty, or access?

Some don't want to imagine it; others are highly invested in the impossibility of it all. But let's just talk about those who crave an end to injustice. Can these well-wishers see it? What does this world look like? What does it feel like? If you can't see it, how do you know when you've achieved it?

The ideal society that the nameless many have fought and died for is a world that many can't imagine. Even those who live the dreams of their predecessors wrestle with leaving familiar notions of identity behind and imagining something new. "There's something about racism that has produced a fatalism that has impacted futuristic thinking," says professor and author Alondra Nelson. While statements like "We don't know what tomorrow will bring" and "The future is not promised" are often said under the guise of well-meaning advice, they have a deeper reach into black diaspora culture, says Nelson. They're countered by the concept of prophecy, she says, or speaking about hope to create a vision for the future. "It's about future thinking, sustainability and imagination."

The imagination is powerful. The narrative of hope that spews from change agents working for social equality is no accident. Dr. Martin Luther King, Rev. Jesse Jackson Sr., even President Barack Obama centered their missions and speeches on hope. On the surface, hope rings as very altruistic—something simple that anyone can do if they just reshuffle their thinking caps or wish upon a star. But the results of a changed mind backed by a bit of empowerment can turn a conflicted world on its head.

Hope, much like imagination, comes at a premium. The cost is a life where more is expected. Where more is expected, new actions are required. The audacity of hope, the bold declaration to believe, and clarity of vision for a better life and world are the seeds to personal growth, revolutionized societies, and life-changing technologies. Desire, hope, and imagination are the cornerstones of social change and the first targets for those who fight against it. "You can't go forward with cynicism—cynicism being disbelief," says Jackson, whose catchphrase "Keep hope alive" may be one of the most popular quotes in modern history. "You have to hope against the odds and not go backwards by fear. Dr. King, Chavez, Gandhi were people who removed people from low places and had the hope," Jackson says.

Imagination, hope, and the expectation for transformative change is a through line that undergirds most Afrofuturistic art, literature, music, and criticism. It is the collective weighted belief that anchors the aesthetic. It is the prism through which some create their way of life. It's a view of the world.

Where there is no vision, the people perish.

Mind Shifting

Taking on this idea of race as a technology sparked new ideas in me. A deliberate by-product of the transatlantic slave trade enforced by violence and law, race (i.e., the division of white and black and the power imbalances based on skin color) simply didn't exist prior to five hundred years ago. I share this in my talks, and I can see the churning of old thoughts and flickers of new ones when audiences begin to see race as a man-made creation.

As a writer who tends to position everything in a cultural context, I was challenged by writing Rayla Illmatic, a character in a completely different world. I wrestled with how to describe characters physically and how to explain their family histories. If your great-grandmother came to a new planet from America, does its history have any context several billion miles away? This stretched my imagination, and this exercise in transcending familiar boundaries is an experience that Afrofuturists seek and encourage. Artist and professor D. Denenge Akpem, an acclaimed ritual-based artist, argues that the artistic process of Afrofuturism itself facilitates personal growth.

Dr. William "Sandy" Darity, a professor of African American history at Duke University, follows me on Twitter. He's a *Rayla* fan, and when he assembled a panel for the Transcending Race conference at Ohio State University, he asked if I would present my ideas on race, based on the *Rayla 2212* project, and predict how it would play out in the far-off future. Others on the panel, including Darity, presented other "what-if" race scenarios, including the impact of a college faculty that reflected the diversity in the country and the impact of a job guarantee on racial inequities. What began as a sci-fi-inspired challenge quickly morphed into a very real issue.

If a new society were created beyond Earth's stratosphere, who would populate it? Would those nations with space programs be the only ones with access to travel to the new world? Is access dependent on the ability to pay for a space flight? With the prospects of commercial endeavors, who has jurisdiction in a dispute? If the colonization of new lands on Earth were any indication, colonization beyond Earth could spur a host of issues.

I presented in spring 2012, the same time that several private companies, including Virgin Galactic, announced their space-tourism ticket sales to the public and a few days shy of the first commercial space flight to the International Space Center. Later, Darity, who is also a sci-fi fan, created the first Race and Space conference to begin in fall 2013 and asked me to join him in launching it. Our initial work in launching the conference came at the same time that former astronaut Mae Jemison, the first black woman to go into space, announced that she'd won a federal grant for the 100 Year Starship project, which is devoted to spurring the necessary technological and social innovations to travel to distant stars. We asked her to be our guest speaker. From creating self-sustaining energy sources to traveling as "DNA slush," the Starship project would leave no stone unturned in the path beyond our solar system. The scientific advancements likely would change new inventions for Earth as well. But the psychological impact of space travel was just as important as the requisite tech savvy. "It'd be unfortunate if the crew didn't make it because they couldn't get along with each other," Jemison said.[1]

Analyzing race as a technology morphed into both an imaginative playground for writing for me but also a very practical tool for real-world space-colonization issues that readers connected with. Just as the actions in the present dictate the future, imagining the future can change the present.

Reenvisioning the Past

The first time I attended a traveling black inventors exhibit, I was awestruck. The "Black Inventions Museum" exhibit was hosted by the DuSable Museum of African American History in Chicago's Washington Park, which, a century prior, was where Cornelius Coffey and John C. Robinson tested their homemade airplane during the first half of the twentieth century. It is also the park Sun Ra frequented when he distributed his self-published inspirational handouts on race, space, and metaphysics while formulating his ideas on the power of music. Nevertheless, my surprise wasn't that black inventors existed. I was familiar with quite a few of their inventions, or so I thought: the traffic light, the refrigerator, the blood bank, the ironing board, the modern-day computer (a frequent jaw-dropper), the Super Soaker, the lawnmower. I'd heard about those before. The shock was the sheer volume of inventions, how they span every aspect of daily life, and their impact on the science world. I didn't know about the space shuttle.

I didn't know that Kenneth Dunkley invented the 3-D glasses I wear at every big-budget blockbuster or that Dr. Philip Emeagwali invented the world's fastest computer. Dr. Shirley Jackson is credited with inventing and contributing to some of the major telecommunications developments of our time, including making advances in the portable fax, touch-tone telephone, solar cells, fiber-optic cables, caller ID, and call waiting—all while she worked at Bell Laboratories. Every time I reach for my smartphone, I have Dr. Jackson to thank.

The list seemed endless. If it's ever in your town, please go see the show.

But the show was so all consuming, even the casual visitor had to wonder, "Is there anything a black man or woman didn't invent?" (Of course there is, but that goes to show how extensive the show was.) I was miffed that I didn't know these people. I was annoyed that when science and technology are discussed, the images of black scientists or inventors don't come to mind. Necessity is the mother of invention, and, historical barriers aside, creation and invention are not determined by skin color. I thought about how empowering it would be for kids of color to know that these inventions were created by people who looked like them. I thought about the importance of the world knowing that people of all walks of life have contributed—and are contributing still—to scientific and technological innovations every day. I thought about the power of ideas and the resilience waged by the imagination.

Part of the Afrofuturist academic's work is uncovering these scientific inventors past and present and incorporating their stories into the larger conversation about science, technology, creativity, and race. Alondra Nelson created the Afrofuturism Listserv in the late 1990s, the first online community devoted to exploring technology and the black experience. Today she writes about African Americans, culture, and science. With her Listserv, she introduced the narrative of hope and imagination and its role amongst black scientists and those who work in the medical field. "I wanted to look at Afrofuturism beyond [just] a lens for looking at music. It's great that there are important figures for looking at Sun Ra and Lee Scratch Perry, but I wanted to push it beyond exploring literature and music. It was about how we can use these insights to think through other kinds of projects, a social science project. For example, how do we get people of color into the STEM fields? Can Afrofuturism, through literature, music, or theory be a way to change prevailing ideas about what science and tech look like?"

Internet Rules

Afrofuturists in the mid-1990s through the mid-2000s were wrestling with the latest game-changing technology of the time, the Internet. The Internet connected global communities, was an information portal, and lowered the barrier of entry to commerce. A small-business owner in Zimbabwe could go global, urban American kids could have unlimited access to information, and people with few resources could get their stories told, documented, and distributed with the click of a mouse . . . that is, if they could afford computers and Internet service. Stories about the digital divide, the percentage of kids of color with computers versus those without, limited broadband in inner-city communities, and lack of computers in urban schools all flooded the media. The urgency led to the creation of conferences on the matter. Between the academic study of the subject and the commercial prospects of an interconnected world, creating equal access to the Internet became a priority for activists and tech companies alike.

The AfroGEEKS conference was held in 2004 and 2005 at the University of California in Santa Barbara. Created by Professor Anna Everett, the conference centered on new media and technological innovation in urban American, Africa, and the African diaspora. Topics included the structural barriers to information technology (IT) access, bloggers and virtual communities, the influence of traditional science education on black youth, high-tech racial surveillance and profiling, and effective models of innovative IT use and adoption.

Conference creators charged that the technology and race debate prioritized the divide at the expense of the ongoing technological innovation in African American communities. "Though rarely represented today as full participants in the information technology revolution, black people are among the earliest adopters and comprise some of the most ardent and innovative users of IT," a statement on the conferences website read. It continued, "It is too often widespread ignorance of African Diasporic people's long history of technology adoption that limits fair and fiscally sound IT investments, policies, and opportunities for black communities locally and globally. Such racially aligned politics of investment create a self-fulfilling prophesy or circular logic wherein the lack of equitable access to technology in black communities produces a corresponding lack of technological literacy and competencies."[2] Everett, along with Amber Wallace, later wrote a book with strategies to encourage advocates, *Afro-GEEKS: Beyond the Digital Divide.*

This question of access underscored the dot-com emergence; it became an issue in the rush to fund the next tech start-up in the vein of Facebook, the creation of new media, and the blogger craze. Suddenly, with the Internet, the cost to reach an audience, sell services, and post information was minimized. Moreover, the use of technology, particularly social media in African American households, outmatched the general population. Over a quarter of all Twitter users in the United States are black.[3] Yet capitalization of tech businesses remains an issue. How could these tools be used to level the playing field? The quest for the answers continues. Although these issues are weighted in practicality, art and literature created in Afrofuturistic veins were obvious inspirations for present-day social change, technology, and the reenvisioning of the future.

Not surprisingly, the Internet and today's technology are actually pushing the ideas in Afrofuturism forward. Gamers, app creators, start-up tech companies, inventors, animators, graphic artists, and filmmakers have faster and cheaper tools at their disposal to use to build and share with the world. The ideas that generate these creations are shared instantly on social media. "I think the movement has evolved," says Stacey Robinson, artist and Afrofuturist, who uses principles of sacred geometry to guide his work. He says, "The technology was the catalyst. I would say it's ironic that technology would forward Afrofuturism. We've talked and theorized about it, but now we can talk to people who feel the way that we do. We can examine the past and theorize the future. Back in the day it would have been Booker T. Washington and W. E. B. Du Bois dominating the conversation on race. But now, someone on the Internet whose name you don't know with an online alias can contribute. I think that's Afrofuturism, that you can recreate a persona online and reinvent yourself with more ease and explore yourself. We're learning about black scientists who are doing things that we have theorized about—inventing things that we have explored and theorized about in our childhood."

MOTHERSHIP

IN THE KEY OF MARS

4

Jazz ingenue and Afrofuturism's founding pillar, eccentric jazz artist Sun Ra, sent an artist-in-residence request to NASA shortly after the dawn of the space age and was rejected. Sun Ra, an Alabama-born musician who claimed Saturn as his mythical home, believed that music and technology could heal and transform the world. He was spellbound by the possibilities of space travel and electric technology. But ideas never die. A half-century later, a pop artist with tech love and Afrofuturistic sensibilities would create a song that Martians could hear.

Hip-hop producer and Black Eyed Peas front man will.i.am has countless musical honors, but none can trump when he debuted "Reach for the Stars" on Mars. "Why do they say the sky is the limit when I've seen the footprints on the moon?" will.i.am sings.

It was the first-ever-planet-to-planet music broadcast in the solar system. In commemoration of the historic landing of NASA's Mars rover *Curiosity*, on August 28, 2012, the song was beamed from Earth to Mars and back—a round trip of some 330 million miles—to an audience of students and scientists at a laboratory in Pasadena, California. Then it was beamed back and played on the Red Planet itself.

The song transmission was will.i.am's idea. NASA administrator Charles Bolden called will.i.am to brainstorm ways to promote NASA to teens. When the artist suggested creating a song aired from the planet, officials asked who would write it.

"I was like, 'Are you guys for real? I'll write the song!'" will.i.am recalled.[1]

Blending traditional musical instruments with the best in beat-making technology, the four-minute song features a forty-piece orchestra matched with techno beats. "This is about inspiring young people to lead a life without limits placed on their potential and to pursue collaboration between humanity and technology," will.i.am said. He hoped that the song would transcend time and culture.

A longtime science lover, will.i.am advocates for STEM Centers, interdisciplinary schools focused on science, technology, engineering, and math, and he's on a mission to inspire children to recognize the technologies around them and use creativity, science, and art to change their environment. "Science and technology [are] already a part of popular culture," will.i.am told a reporter shortly after the broadcast. "The world of STEM hasn't found a way to remind people that iPod and iPad and all the code that makes Twitter and Facebook work all comes from people who have an education around STEM," he said.

"I don't want my neighborhood to continue to be the way it was twenty years from now," he said. "All it takes is one kid, one kid from Boyle Heights, to be Mark Zuckerberg, and my neighborhood's changed forever."[2]

But will.i.am isn't the only musician working with NASA. CopperWire, an Ethiopian hip-hop group tapped the nation's scientists to collect sonified light curves, or sounds from stars, that they're mixing in their new app. In April 2012 the group debuted their album *Earthbound*. Raising funds on Kickstarter, a popular crowdsourcing site, the group's accompanying app will also include an augmented reality space-flight game, an interactive art widget and comic book, unreleased songs, artwork, and playable instruments.

"The idea of making music from a galactic perspective gives you the opportunity to make up an entire world for sound to exist in," says Burntface, the CopperWire member who's also the 3-D modeler and graphic designer behind the group's Phone Home remix Android app.[3] The app's algorithms can generate two million variations of the song based on any ten-digit phone number.

Soundtrack to the Future

Afrofuturists value universal love, reinterpret sound and technology, and echo beauties of a lost past as the essence of a harmonious future. While the music is full of mind-benders, with the new era of technology, sounds can literally go beyond the stratosphere. Always ahead of the curve, Afrofuturist music embodies the times while literally sounding out of this world. Listen to Sun Ra's "Astro Black," Lee Scratch Perry's "Disco Devil," Brides of Funkenstein's "Mother May I?," an X-ecutioners live DJ show, "Drexciya's 2 Hour Mix—Return to Bubble Metropolis" by VLR, and "Dance of the Pseudo Nymph" by Flying Lotus and you too might feel like you've been sailing on a black ark from a distant star.

But the music is about more than good vibes. Physicist and musician Stephon Alexander revealed in a TED talk that jazz legend John Coltrane's song "Giant Steps" was an aural and physical diagram of Einstein's Theory of Relativity. Alexander stumbled upon a diagram by Coltrane and realized it plotted out geometrical theories of quantum gravity and matched the notes and chord changes in the song. The discovery sparked other research on the parallels between music and quantum physics, and Alexander and his team learned that the Western scale of music also resembles the double helix of DNA.

"It's outrageous," says James Haile, philosopher and organizer of the 2013 Black Existentialism Conference held at Duquesne

University. Haile watched Alexander's talk and was floored by the links between music and quantum theory. "It might be the most fascinating thing I've ever heard," he said. "I had an idea that's what was going on, but to have a trained physicist prove that shows it's more than a notion." What do such discoveries mean for Afrofuturists? "It shows how we can incorporate particle physics into Afrofuturism and coordinate ideas three dimensionally," says Haile. As for the world at large, the discovery gives new depth to the power of music.

"Afrofuturistic music is music that pushes beyond the norms and standards of our current culture," says Leon Q. Allen, composer and trumpet player. Leon Q. fuses Latin jazz and house music to create futuristic expressions of both. He contributed to the *Rayla 2212* soundtrack and is also a member of the legendary AACM, a world-renowned avant-garde collective inspired by Sun Ra that emphasizes sonic healing. "It's the 'what next' factor," Leon says of Afrofuturist music. "It's music that's moving forward to a new place of cultural significance."

Afrofuturism is the only future-oriented aesthetic that has such a rich history in music. George Clinton, Sun Ra, Bootsy Collins, Jimi Hendrix, Lee Scratch Perry, Grace Jones, LaBelle, Outkast, Erykah Badu, Janelle Monáe, X-ecutioners, funk, dub, turntablism, soundclash, Detroit techno, Chicago house, even Coltrane and Miles Davis, have all been framed in an Afrofuturistic context— music that shifted the edge. Whether through lyrics of inspiration, new technologies in music, or shock-and-awe performances, the idea of music and in some cases black identity and gender identity evolved. "The approach is not limited to a certain style of music, the approach is based on the desire," says Leon Q. "People have to study what's going on in the society and the culture and look at the trends and patterns for what's going on at the time."

The desire to be more, to be free of the constrictions of a society with marked color distinctions and separation is like pixie dust sprinkled throughout the tracks. The music echoes with a universalism rhythmically that emanates from the roots of African music but is jet-fueled into the future. There are no barriers in Afrofuturist music, no entity that can't emit a rhythmic sound, no arrangements to adhere to, no locked-in structures about chorus and verse. Wordplay is keen.

The standards are high. "When you line up everything that has come before you—if you line up Muddy Waters, Jimi Hendrix, Miles Davis, all the way up to now and imagine yourself standing in front of them—are you contributing something that is equal in weight?" asks Morgan Craft, an electric guitarist who has played with Meshell Ndegeocello, among others. "You have to push something that is equal to what the masters have pushed before you. If you don't hold yourself up to their standard, it's a waste of time."

However, if there's a cosmic ground floor for the existence of Afrofuturism in music, Sun Ra and George Clinton would be that foundation. The idea of a song mythology from the cosmos, high-flying African-inspired space costumes, wordplay that challenged logic, and the use of traditional and electronic instruments to redefine sounds and push for universal love were established by Sun Ra and George Clinton. Both are referenced more than any other artist as the inspiration for today's Afrofuturists. Clinton, whose funk sounds came to the forefront in the 1970s, later spoke of being inspired by Sun Ra, who began creating sonar sounds for the space age in the '50s.

While many Afrofuturist artists have donned the space gear and metallic pants of the musical space cadet, in the case of those artists dubbed as Afrofuturist innovators, the space theme was more than just a kooky gimmick to play off the space age, more than an eyebrow-raising marketing ploy. The colorful, albeit shiny, costumes served as a visual tool to stimulate higher thinking and to prepare audiences for something new.

In other cases, the costuming wasn't a focal point at all. Creative uses of technological innovations to create reigned queen. The wordplay, the heights of irony and dissonance, compelled listeners to question their take on reality. "What I appreciated about Parliament, Funkadelic, and Sun Ra is that they were almost speaking in code. Almost like the old Negro spirituals, we're going to talk about three things in this one line, and you almost have to be in the club to understand," says Shawn Wallace, composer and arranger, noting that the best in hip-hop lyricism uses the same layered language.

Afrofuturists enjoy challenging their listeners on their path to enlightenment. They enjoy pulling the rug out from under the smugness of reality. Whether it's through chord arrangements, oddity, or sheer boldness, they get a kick out of tossing their listeners into the far reaches of outer space.

The Trifecta: Sun Ra, George Clinton, and Lee Scratch Perry

When Sun Ra, born Herman Poole Blount, left Birmingham, Alabama, for Chicago in the late 1940s, he was already a well-respected jazz musician with extraordinary talents. But his affection for electronic music and predictions that man would one day land on the moon made him stand apart. "He was very well read," said Arthur Hoyle, renowned jazz artist who played with Sun Ra in the late '50s. In a time when Chicago's South Side was littered with jazz bands and clubs, Sun Ra was a fixture on the scene. Before he adopted the flashlights, solar helmets, and sci-fi African garb that would come to be his trademark, he was known as one of the most scholarly musicians around and would frequently hand out literature about his theories in Washington Park. His canon of must-reads included books on theosophy, numerology, metaphysics, science fiction, biblical studies, and a glut of underground alternative history books and African history books. He was propelled to answer what others hadn't questioned and gravitated to books with theories on the origins of the world that differed from the Eurocentric lessons propagated in media and schools.

Sun Ra wanted to use music to heal. He had a preacher-like conversion moment. Part spiritual revelation, part self-described alien encounter, Sun Ra believed he came to the world to heal. This quest to fill the knowledge gaps, to find the erased contributions of people of color, and to ultimately shatter the color/class divides resulted in an information trek that would last for much of his life. And this searching for more, this desire to know the answers that weren't readily available in the classics and media of the time, was the impetus for his stretch in music. Although he was adept at playing the big band and bebop that defined jazz in the 1950s and early '60s, he did not want to be limited by its form. He named himself Sun Ra after the Egyptian sun deity and claimed he was from Saturn.

Sun Ra was a total original. He was a founding father of Afrofuturism, a pioneer of electronic music, playing multiple electronic keyboards long before anyone in jazz or otherwise adopted the instrument. Moreover, he was a forerunner of today's space-music genre, new-age or ambient electronica designed for contemplation.

"He had a very original concept that was way beyond his time," says Nicole Mitchell, avant-garde jazz flutist and composer who met Sun Ra when she was twenty. "He was one of the first African Americans to start his own record companies and was one of the first jazz artists to incorporate African percussion as well as improvising electronics into his music. He wanted to find the real power of music," she says, noting that he also believed music could develop telepathy.

With so many ideas to explore, space analogies were the ideal way for Sun Ra to escape the parameters of music and humanity, and they freed him creatively to ponder the life questions he seemed so dedicated to answering and addressing through music. Hyperlinking his music to space travel created a prism of creativity for Sun Ra. He explored with healing tones, new sounds, and pushed jazz beyond its bebop dimensions. Songs like "Astro Black," "Nubia," and "Dance of the Cosmo Alien" explored cosmic origins and sonically both abided and broke the rules of modern jazz simultaneously.

Arthur Hoyle played with Sun Ra in Chicago before leaving to travel with Lionel Hampton. He shared a story about how the two reconnected in New York shortly after Sun Ra moved there in 1961. Sun Ra and his Arkestra came up the steps in their space-aged garb and elaborate wired headgear. The combination of shield-like metal ornaments caused the motley crew to clank with every step. A neighbor peered into the hall and shut her door immediately. "She probably thought they were from outer space," Hoyle said. While Sun Ra claimed he was from Saturn, he created a cosmology for himself and his music that rooted its eccentricities in a land beyond the stratosphere.

Sun Ra was also a showman, and the theatrical costumes combined with the music was a one-two punch that would come to define the assault on the senses that many musical artists in Afrofuturism would use as a model. Sometimes he drew his own album covers. He was also a fervent poet. By the time he moved to New York in 1961, he sported his onstage garb daily, walking the streets of Harlem with his Arkestra of Saturn-born ingenues. The band lived, ate, and created music together while immersing themselves in Sun Ra's philosophy and synergizing their unique approach. Anyone in conversation with him, during rehearsal breaks and elsewhere, was either held hostage or caught spellbound by his verbal debates and attempts to solve the mysteries of the world.

In 1974 Sun Ra starred in the cult classic *Space Is the Place*, an independent feature film directed by John Coney. An incredibly magical film that underscores the quagmires of self-determination, backed by Sun Ra's effervescent piano solos and rhythmic big band space music, *Space Is the Place* is named after one of Ra's most popular songs. The story follows Sun Ra's earthly return and attempt to convince African Americans to leave Earth and embark on a new life on a distant planet with different vibrations and "under different stars."

The film opens on this lush planet world. Sun Ra sits in a multihued garden in his new colony wearing Egyptian sphinx head garb and states that time is officially over. He "works on the other side of time," he adds. He then concludes that he would bring the black populace to this world "through isotope, tele-portation, transmoleculization or, better still, teleport the whole planet here through music." Sun Ra then travels back in time to his early musical haunts and must contest with proverbial free-dom gatekeepers, including a pimp named the Overseer, while embarking on his quest to transport the race to the far-off space colony with music. The film defies categorization, but Sun Ra's celebration of the unity of life is clear. "Yes, you're music too," he states. "We're all instruments. Everyone is supposed to be play-ing their part in this vast arkestra of the cosmos." *Space Is the Place* creates a rich world to understand Sun Ra's sensory-altering sounds while conveying his purpose as a musician.

Although Sun Ra received critical success and attracted a loyal fan base around the world, he was never a chart topper. Yet hundreds of musicians came under his tutelage. One of Sun Ra's prized musicians, Kelan Phil Cohran, was inventor of the Frankiephone, an electronic kalimba also known as the Space Harp and featured on several Sun Ra albums. Cohran was Mau-rice White's music teacher. White would later found the R&B band Earth, Wind & Fire, known for their songs of peace and love as well as their space-inspired, Egyptian-themed costumes.

Shortly after Sun Ra's death in 1993, Afrofuturism was born.

Funk to the Future

George Clinton also reframed the soul music of the time, chal-lenging James Brown's band's tight funk with fluid chords and repetitive bass lines by former Brown bandmates Bootsy and Cat-fish Collins. They created funk, a syrupy, bass-heavy music form designed to create states of ecstasy akin to the trance conscious-ness that morphs from tribal drumming, but using a mid-tempo bass guitar as the match. The sound would shape the 1970s and influence music into the twenty-first century. "JB brought you to an elevated state of consciousness. Parliament/Funkadelic brought you to an altered state of consciousness," says Leon Q.

Clinton said that at the time he created funk, blackness itself had become commercial. "I had to find another place where they hadn't perceived black people to be and that was on a space-ship," he said in the 1996 documentary *The Last Angel of History.*[4] Parliament's fourth album, *Mothership Connection*, shows a sunglasses-wearing, metallic-silver-clad Clinton coming out of or entering a flying saucer. The mothership came from the star Sirius, harking back to the Dogon's theory of origin. Clinton was a Newark-raised barber from North Carolina whose early doo-wop group the Parliaments tapped into the late 1960s' societal transformation. Looking to Sly Stone and Jimi Hendrix and their fusion of R&B and psychedelic rock, the mothership became a bridge between a missing African past and a glorious space-age future.

Funk, as Clinton envisioned it, aspired to free minds, using dancing, a heartbeat-like bass line, irony and metaphors, theat-rics, and liberation-tinged space metaphors. In a sense, Clinton and his bands created astral-liberation party music.

"What that really stood for in black culture was the exuber-ance of craziness," says Leon Q. "It was the embracing of the chaos. It had as much chaos as it did uniformity."

But like Sun Ra, funk also celebrated universalism and one-ness in humanity. Clinton took Sun Ra's concepts and made them a part of pop culture. "Everyone wanted to be on this level that was higher than the Earth. It's like his music was going to take you to space," says Leon Q. Like Sun Ra, Clinton was a forerunner in electronic instruments. "George Clinton's approach was, 'How can we make this music sound beyond our time, taking the music to the next level on a sonic and psychoanalytic level?'" The concept caught like wildfire.

Parliament and Funkadelic and their funkateer offshoots had chart-topping hits like "One Nation Under a Groove," "Flash Light," and "Mothership Connection." Today these bands are touted as two of the greatest of all time and were co-inducted into the Rock and Roll Hall of Fame as Parliament/Funkadelic in 1997. "This whole thing about the funk being cosmic, it made people desire to be cosmic. It made people want to educate themselves on these concepts. Everybody was listening to George Clinton. Everyone wanted to be on the mothership. People wanted to push forward and move beyond their time," said Leon Q. Some, including the creators, used drugs to induce this state, but the music was high enough.

Parliament and Funkadelic were two different bands, with shared members, each reflecting the visions of Clinton. Parliament focused on more polished commercial releases and Funkadelic delved into a complicated story and loosely formatted groove structure with psychedelic rock appeal. Dr. Funkenstein, a Clinton alter ego in Parliament, came from outer space to teach earthlings the funk. Parliament's concerts began opening with a giant spaceship landing on stage and a dance party of space-themed musicians and dancers devoted to bringing the funk.

Parliament/Funkadelic's wordplay was equally fascinating. Even the word funk had a duel meaning. "P-Funk seemed to believe that music wasn't so much something that you made with your instruments as it was something that you caught with them, as if funk was out there in the form of an ambient residual energy left over from the big bang," says Scot Hacker, author of "Can You Get to That? The Cosmology of P-Funk."[5]

Playing on a list of double entendres and ironic metaphors, nearly everything they said meant the opposite of what it implied. Although this multisymbolic wordplay made for clever quips and new slang, it was a verbal assault on the senses, inferring that all is never quite what it seems. What's up is down, what's hot is cold . . . all newfound slang that subtly made listeners who paid attention question the reality of things. Up until the time of George Clinton, a lot of the slang words came out of the jazz world, says Leon Q.

As for the mothership, the metaphor is used in songs spanning R&B and hip-hop, with Erykah Badu reminding people that "the mothership can't save you" in her song "On and On." Outkast's *ATLiens* album drew from P-Funk album-cover imagery. The samples of funk in West Coast G-funk by the likes of Dr. Dre and beyond redefined hip-hop music and generated millions from samples alone.

The Black Ark

Lee Scratch Perry is one of the leading reggae producers and mixers, defining the sound for reggae and later dub. His single "People Funny Boy," recorded in 1968, included an early act of sampling—of a crying baby—and defined the reggae sound. In the documentary on his life, *The Upsetter*, he said he created the reggae sound to reinterpret the swinging motion of workers with pickaxes hitting rocks along the Jamaican countryside.

Perry created the dub sound in the mid-1970s by layering the same sounds on top of one another, initially playing the same sound on two tape players and recording it. The dub classic "Disco Devil" uses a range of layering and ambient sounds never before used. Perry's unique production techniques are the basis for modern reggae and its derivatives today. In 1973 he built the Black Ark, his own production studio, where he produced Bob Marley and the Wailers, Max Romeo, and the Congos among others. The songs spread the virtues of peace and love and revolution. Perry was later recruited to work with British punk, rock, and ska bands in the 1990s and 2000s.

Study My Track

Sun Ra, George Clinton, and Lee Scratch Perry have inspired not just musical genres, but critical music writing that explores their technological approach to sound.

"Funk music is the perfect way to explain Afrofuturism," says Guillaume Dupit. Dupit, a French-born musician, wrote his doctoral music thesis on funk and Clinton. Immersed in the French jazz scene, he was intrigued by funk's creation. He compares the repetition in funk to the laced sampling in hip-hop as a machine-meets-man duality. "It's like if you take a sample, the same way you can in hip-hop, you play it and play it, and repeat it," he says. "In the composition of the funk, you take a sample and you play it thirty minutes or four hours with instruments. A lot of their songs have the same construction. The same drumbeat, just small variations. And yet, the idea of repetition in funk is machine-like."

He continues, "You can't reproduce the notion of the groove with a machine. If you take the same sample and repeat it, it's not the same result if you play it with instruments. It's like science fiction, this balance between the machine and human. I think the point of replaying a sample with an instrument, something that can be relayed by a machine is really specific and hard to replicate. When you see Bootsy Collins playing his bass, it's not playing soul or jazz or rock. It's like a machine playing a sample, with micro variations and a totally different feel.

"They create something that the machine can't reproduce. Machines are supposed to do that. Machines are supposed to take a sample and replay it, but the results aren't the same," says Dupit.

Unlike Sun Ra, whose global trek never crossed pop-chart thresholds, Clinton's funk creation launched both a new musical genre and commercial success. "I'm amazed that he could talk about these concepts and be so successful," says Nicole Mitchell.

Electric Boogaloo

Many musicians hailing from the funk era of the 1970s and the jazz and blues scenes that preceded it—despite their own experimentation with synthesizers and other electronic instruments—were not fans of disco, nor were they in love with the shift to electronic-based music that prompted writer Nelson George to declare the late 1980s and beyond the "post-soul" era.

The hail of scratchology, sampling, and break beats that defined early New York hip-hop along with the Euro-inspired beat-machine-riddled rhythms in house and techno surfacing from black neighborhoods in Chicago, Detroit, and Baltimore was ushered in with as much criticism as praise in the '80s. The very construction of the music—the use of record players as an instrument and the notion of using a speaking voice over an isolated beat—was fresh and highly criticized by music impresarios.

But rather than seeing electronic music as the death of soul and funk, Afrofuturist and music writer Kodwo Eshun believes this machine-era transition is a foray into the depths of how humans can experience music. "Where critics of CyberCult still gather, 99.9% of them will lament the disembodiment of the human by technology," writes Eshun. "But machines don't distance you from your emotions, in fact, quite the opposite. Sound machines make you feel more intensely, along a broader band of emotional spectra than ever before in the 20th Century."[6]

Eshun introduced the idea that the emergence of electronic music, beginning with the use of the synthesizer in jazz and R&B and eventually the pulse effects of house to Detroit techno and hip-hop turntablism, launched a new space for sound and music. This music is not a continuation of a lineage but rather the beginning of music into the future. Although Eshun argues that music by black artists tends to be written in a historical and biographical context, this digitized uprising in music encompassed a host of fresh sounds and ideas in music that had never been created before, a concept that he dubs "Alien Music."

Eshun describes Alien Music in his book *More Brilliant Than the Sun* as "the distance between Tricky and what you took to be the limits of black music, the gap between Underground Resistance and what you took Black Music to be."[7] These sounds don't have a language, and the layman's terms used to describe both music-making machines and the spaces they inhabit are inadequate. The drum machine, he argues, does not mimic a drum but is rather a rhythm synthesizer that resequences patterns.

Eshun compares the break beat, the skeleton of hip-hop, to motion capture. He writes, "They grabbed a beat which was always there, by severing it from the funk engine, by materializing it as an actual piece of the vinyl that could be repeated." Eventually, variations of this music would dominate the mainstream, and the history of the music would be placed in the musical lineage of soul like James Brown and the oral traditions before it.

Flying Lotus is one such artist. Born Steven Ellison, he is the grandnephew of jazz artists Alice and John Coltrane and grandson of songwriter Marilyn McLeod, who penned Diana Ross's disco classic "Love Hangover." With some musical shoes to fill, Flying Lotus continues to build on electronic music, creating both ambient and emotional music. He uses turntables, samplers, drum machines, and keyboards. His ethereal rhythms have some jazz inflections, are rarely accompanied by vocals, and are distinct in their creation of a completely digital music space. While some completely electronic music creations try to mimic other sounds and instruments, Flying Lotus albums from *1983* to *Until the Quiet Comes* rely purely on the dynamics of the digital realm to create a new form of intimate listening.

Space Is the Place

Although many Afrofuturists use space metaphors, space itself often literally means creating a new place to anchor unique sounds.

Drexciya, a Detroit-reared duo consisting of James Stinson and Gerald Donald, developed a mythology to orient their subterranean techno sounds. Borrowing Sun Ra and George Clinton's concept of creating a musical cosmology, the duo created a new myth of a Drexciyan race. The Drexciyans are an underwater nation, the descendants of the African women thrown overboard in the transatlantic slave trade. With songs like "Hydro Theory" and "Andreaen Sand Dunes," the duo, who only appeared masked in public, created a fluid sound and became techno pioneers.

DJ Spooky has long been fascinated with the process of creating music, often incorporating his skills into multimedia presentations. His famous *Rebirth of a Nation* showcase saw him sync his turntable with the footage from the film *The Birth of a Nation* and remix the film—known for its modern technology and racist imagery—live, with aural sounds and mixology. Recently, DJ Spooky has created and experimented with using apps to deejay music live and create songs. His latest project, *Sinfonia Antarctica*, led the New York DJ to travel to Antarctica with a portable studio, where he captured the acoustic qualities of the ice forms and created a seventy-minute suite speaking to the region's environmental stress.

Inspired by British composer Ralph Vaughan Williams's 1952 composition titled *Sinfonia Antartica* (a difference of just one C), DJ Spooky takes Williams's ode to the continent, which he never visited, and adds some icy reality. "Think of it as sampling the environment with sound—something that Vaughan could only do with metaphor [when he was writing] in 1949," writes DJ Spooky.

Sonic Orchestras

Musical technology isn't limited to computers. There's a technology in the practice that live musicians embrace too.

Nicole Mitchell, critically acclaimed Afrofuturist flutist and composer, was equally influenced by sci-fi writer Octavia Butler and jazz pioneer Sun Ra. The daughter of a sci-fi writer and painter—"I grew up with images of a sunrise on another planet on my wall," she says—she learned jazz improvisation while in college. "When I learned [improvisation] I wanted to go on the street and play a soundtrack for everyone who walked by," she once said.

She later helmed the Black Earth Ensemble and became the first woman president of the AACM, where she learned how to use music for sonic healing and the use of indigenous instruments in jazz. Her release *Xenogenesis Suite: A Tribute to Octavia Butler,* was commissioned by Chamber Music America's New Jazz Works program in 2010. Mitchell says, "I had a chance to interview [Butler] at the 2006 Black Writers Conference. I said, Wouldn't it be amazing to create music around her work? I wanted to collaborate." However, the day Mitchell mailed off the proposal, Butler passed away.

"I decided that no matter what, I wanted to do this project," Mitchell says. The experience pushed Mitchell to alter her music-writing style. She employed singers to sing without using words and envisioned sounds that took her beyond the scale.

"I can write pretty traditional scores, but in this piece I wrote a graphic score as a way to get the real expression out for the musicians. I just didn't want it written out note for note. Not only did it use traditional musical notation, but also using drawings, and poetry to get what I needed." Although she had worked with most of the musicians for a while, the approach often went "against their intuition to get what I wanted," she says.

She continues, "I might want the saxophonist to make bird sounds. Writing out bird sounds would not be as fluid, if they were trying to read some crazy high notes, so I gave them a picture and a graphic of what I was looking for. It's just about finding the most effective way to communicate with the musicians and sometimes you have to get off the page."

Guitar Revelations

Guitarist Morgan Craft was born in Minnesota. He grew up on heavy metal and hard rock and gravitated to early 1990s black rock bands like Living Colour. "Vernon Reid was the sun I revolved around," he jokes. But Greg Tate's writing "Star Black Rise" introduced him to the idea of Afrofuturism and gave Craft a voice for the innovation he craved.

Pointing to the AACM as well as the technology in music today, Craft feels that some artists are holding themselves back to maintain a framework that no longer fits. "When I look out there at what is being pushed on us as black music and the box that it's in right now, I can't help but think that we're way beyond that now. It seems natural for futuristic black music to embrace all of our potentialities," he says. "If we don't have anything that is taking us into the future, where are we going to go? We can't go back to blues anymore. We have cameras and megapixels today. When blues was created, you had a guitar and one string. We have to be concerned with futurism."

Currently, Craft is living in Italy with his wife, who is a turntablist. His latest music exploration is "breaking the sound barrier," he says. "When you think of music in the West like pop and rock, the frame of that music is based on twelve notes, the chromatic scale. Those twelve notes are cool; it gave us a lot of cool music, but is that all there is? If I drop a spoon, it might not be one of those twelve notes. But what if I make the sound of that spoon? You can use any sound and build music from it." Noting that Mahalia Jackson and the famous blues musicians played "blue notes," or notes between the scale, Craft says there are a host of sounds we're just not exploring.

"When you think about all the great music that came from the twelve notes of the chromatic scale, all the music we dig today comes from twelve notes. I'm not saying get rid of those twelve notes. I love what music has done and what it will be. But as a musician who is concerned about music, I say, what's beyond those twelve notes?"

Jimi Hendrix's use of reverb on the guitar is viewed in Afrofuturistic terms as the use of new sound. "If you have an electric guitar and it's loud, you will hear some crazy sounds," says Craft. "Jimi Hendrix did it with feedback. It's not the idea of notes, but beyond those notes we have sound. If you go to school, they teach you theory about an A major chord, C major, based on the chromatic scale, which are technically numbers. They're telling us that music is really math. It seemed to me that when you listen to music, you're not thinking about trigonometry or anything, you're just feeling it. It dawned on me, music is not about math, and it's about sound." Is there an undiscovered world of music with sounds we've yet to utilize?

"It's an art form you can't see. It's aural. It's sonic. If it's sonic and emotional, can't you take any sound and get it to speak? Instead of playing the guitar like Jimi, you take a bread knife and take it up and down a string, put it on a floor and step on it. You can make all these crazy sounds, but can you get them to communicate? The challenge for futuristic invention is to get new sounds to communicate."

Androids Rising

Janelle Monáe is a modern-day musical paradox. Sporting a coiffed 1950s pompadour and snug tuxedo, the Kansas-born singer's futuristic sound is rich with romance-craving droids and time travel. She was discovered by Outkast's Big Boi, another Afrofuturistic point person, who introduced her to Bad Boy Records' Sean Combs, arguably hip-hop's greatest marketer. Monáe's music, look, and frenetic dance channel James Brown, *Stankonia*, big-band-era Duke Ellington, and the best in uplifting sonic sound. Her shock-and-awe demeanor and masculine façade are a visual shout-out to Grace Jones. Her powerful vocals evoke memories of jazz greats.

Her music has a story.

Monáe's alter ego, Cindi Mayweather, is a silver metallic-dipped android sent to "free the citizens of Metropolis from the Great Divide," a secret society using time travel to suppress freedom and love throughout the ages. When the ArchAndroid returns, the android community will be free. The space saga includes love, revolution, and heroism, complete with an android uprising, freedom fights, and ultimate peace.

Metropolis combines such a wide array of time periods, sounds, layers, and intrigue that it feels like audio time travel. Even the music's mythology has a mythology. Monáe likes to say that her tunes are created at the "Palace of Dogs," a place that cannot be spoken of.

Monáe, too, uses traditional orchestra instruments courtesy of the Wondaland ArchOrchestra as well as kinetic computer-generated beats.

Just in case the purpose of these hyperlayered metaphors and musical arrangements goes over your head, Monáe distributes the Ten Droid Commandments at her concert. Written like P-Funk hyperbole, the commandments instruct attendees on how to experience the music.

Commandment 4: "Please be aware that the songs you will hear are electric: be careful as you experience them and interact with electrical devices, drink water or touch others. The Wondaland Arts Society will not be held responsible for melted telecommunications devices or injuries resulting from lockback, sweat-tech, leaveweave, poparm, shockjaw, electrobutt, or any other maladies or malfunctions caused by the jam."

Commandment 6: "Abandon your expectations about art, race, gender, culture and gravity."

Commandment 7: "Before the show, feel free to walk about the premises impersonating one of the many inspirations of the ArchanDroid Emotion Picture: (Choose One) Salvador Dali, Walt Disney, Outkast, Stevie Wonder, Octavia Butler, David Bowie, Andy Warhol or John Williams."

Commandment 9: "By shows end you must transform. This includes, but is not limited to, eye colour, perspective, mood or height."[8]

Like her Afrofuturistic brethren before her, including Sun Ra who donned a flashlight or cosmic crown, and George Clinton's multicolored hair and space suit, Monáe is rarely, if ever, seen without her starched shirt, pompadour, and classic shrunken tux. At the 2012 Black Girls Rock! Awards, she said her costume was an ode to her working-class parents, who wore uniforms too.

The song "Q.U.E.E.N" from the *Electric Lady* album includes fellow Afrofuturist Erykah Badu. In the video, the two are suspended in animation in a future's past museum exhibit on rebels who used music as a freedom movement. The song, a funk throwback, is an ode to the eccentric, independent ladies of the world who are labeled as freaks for being themselves.

Monáe has an ArchOrchestra; Sun Ra had an Arkestra. Sun Ra came from Saturn to teach earthlings how to love; Cindi Mayweather must return to free her robotic counterparts. Sun Ra juggernauts to space using African themes, Monáe hyperlinks back to the '50s big-band jazz era in which Sun Ra cultivated his cosmos theories. Monáe was mentored in part by unconventional hip-hop duo Outkast, which featured Andre 3000—as in the year 3000. Outkast borrowed their stylistics from P-Funk themes, most notably their *Stankonia* music in honor of the funk.

The mothership is in flight.

HERE COMES... THE MIGHTY PHANTASM

5

THE AFRICAN COSMOS
FOR MODERN MERMAIDS
(MERMEN)

r. Malidoma Patrice Somé is a scholar and noted shaman of the Dagara, a society in Ghana and Burkina Faso that has maintained ancient practices. Somé is most popular for documenting his journey to shamanism in the 1994 book *Of Water and the Spirit: Ritual, Magic, and Initiation in the Life of an African Shaman*. He writes about the proverbial dive into the rabbit hole as he was studying with the elders of his community and balancing his newfound wisdom with his Western education. Somé paints a picture of a different path to knowledge that contradicts the norms of Western conventions. According to him, the Dagara have no word for the supernatural. "For us, as for many indigenous cultures, the supernatural is part of our everyday lives," he writes. The Dagara also don't draw a line between reality and imagination either, he writes, but rather emphasize the power of thought to create reality.[1]

And the Dagara don't have a word for fiction. Out of curiosity, Somé decided to conduct an experiment. In the book, he recalls a day in 1996 when he showed the film *Star Trek* to his shaman elders. The elders watched the film, assuming that these were the day-to-day happenings of a group in another part of the world. He writes, "My elders were comfortable with *Star Trek*, the West's vision of its own future. Because they believe in things like magical beings (Spock), traveling at the speed of light, and teleportation, the wonders that Westerners imagine being part of their future are very much a part of my elders' present. The irony is that the West sees the indigenous world as primitive or archaic. Wouldn't it be wonderful if the West could learn to be as 'archaic' as my elders are?"[2]

But the elders also found the Trekster spaceship and outfits to be a bit cumbersome in the magic-making process. It would be much simpler if they just traveled with their minds.

The absence of Africa's contribution to global knowledge in history, science, and beyond is a gaping hole so expansive it almost feels like a missing organ in the planet's cultural anatomy. Can humanity ever know itself with this rigid segmentation of knowledge? Can ancient knowledge be recovered? Can trauma be erased? While the whys and hows that led to this void are etched in history, the obvious absence has compelled many Afrofuturists to look to the continent's myths, spirituality, and art on a never-ending quest for wholeness.

Afrofuturist artists site Egyptian deities, the Dogon myths, water myths, and Yoruba orishas more than any other African cosmology in their art, music, and literature. From the costumes of Earth, Wind & Fire to Lee Scratch Perry's Black Ark to the idea of the mothership itself, the Dogon's star bond with Sirius and ancient Egyptians' unexplained technologies are the basis for Afrofuturist lore, art, and spectacle.

These cultures are referenced largely because of the sci-fi elements and mysticism in the mythology. The Egyptian and Dogon, in particular, are the most documented African wisdoms in the world. The importance of the Yoruba orishas and African water deities to enslaved African cultures in the Americas resound with descendants and continental Africa today. Afrofuturists are intrigued by Africa's ancient wisdom and ancient wisdom from around the world. The aesthetic attracts students of the esoteric. Shamanism, metaphysics, Hinduism, Buddhism, African traditional religions, mystical Christianity, Sufism, Native American spirituality, astrology, martial arts mythology, and other ancient wisdoms are typically funneled through an African or diasporic viewpoint.

Stargazing is a popular pastime.

"Afrofuturism is about looking at and recovering those ancient ways and looking at how artists through the '60s and now are using those to talk about the future," says D. Denenge Akpem, scholar and performance artist.

Ancient Egypt and Nubia

Afrofuturists love to anchor their work in golden eras from times long gone, and there's no ancient culture that merges the heights of science and the esoteric like the Egyptians and Nubians. Egypt's reign in the ancient world and Nubia's influence stand as proof that cultures of dark-skinned people ruled advanced societies and shaped global knowledge.

From naming themselves after Egyptian deities to donning the wardrobe, no stone is left unturned in the quest to reinterpret the greatness of ancient Egypt and Nubia in modern and futuristic black cultures. Ankhs, pharaoh crowns, and snakes are the visual aesthetic of the pharoahs. Gods and goddesses reappear in Afrofuturistic art, depicting an Egyptian cosmology that is as much in the past as it is the future.

Ancient Egypt's stellar deities Ra, Isis, Horus, Set, the sky goddess Nut, and beyond are common mythological inspirations. Sun Ra named himself after the Egyptian god, and Erykah Badu gained fame while wearing the Egyptian ankh—a symbol of eternal life and fertility—in videos and stage shows, which repopularized African-inspired fashion and piqued curiosity about quantum physics.

But Afrofuturists aren't the only ones reeled in by Egypt's glory. The Egyptian Book of the Dead, the mysteries of the pyramids and Sphinx, even the love-drenched tales of Cleopatra have inspired some of the greatest art, motion pictures, and literature of our time. Although anthropologists continue to crack away at the time-honored mysteries of the ancient Egyptians, the true meanings behind their mythology, architecture, religion, and writings are still cloaked in question marks, inspiring speculative history and theories that zigzag straight to space. Ancient Egypt is a treasure trove of speculation. Writers have speculated that the pyramids are celestial portals to other worlds. Others say that aliens, not humans, are the true architect, a theory often fraught with racism for its inability to imagine brown-skinned people achieving such mastery. Then there's also the speculation that Egyptians had a special connection to other worlds. Even the blockbuster film *Prometheus* implies that the hieroglyphics are the offshoots of an ancient alien language.

In 1787 Count C. Volney, French scholar and author of *Ruins of Empires*, delighted readers with the wonders and impact of Egyptian culture on the changing world and the intellect of the "black-skinned" creators.

Early Egyptian libraries and secret societies were the envy of philosophers from Pythagoras to Plato, both of whom studied in Egypt. How did this culture come to be? What secrets did it hold? What were its secret teachings? Ancient Egyptian culture and lore is as much a pipeline to the great beyond as the mystery of dark matter.

The Afrofuturistic claim on the culture places the nation at the heart of African diaspora history, a statement that counters popular culture's tendency to divorce Egypt from its African locale and people. "A lot cling on to it because it is a high point in

African history," says Afua Richardson, comic illustrator, about ancient Egypt's popularity among Afrofuturists. "The pyramids themselves are one of the great mysteries of the world."

An artist in a family of scientists, Richardson began her career as a flutist, playing for Sheila E. and Parliament/Funkadelic, among others, and was soon asked to lend her artistic skills to create album covers for Nona Hendryx. Richardson is a fan of speculative fiction on ancient societies and is developing a new comic on the Egyptian mystery schools and technology. However, Egyptian imagery in Afrofuturism is so popular it's almost cliche, and she wants to add a new spin. "I want to combine futuristic imagery with shamanism," she says.

Others look to the culture's realities as a backdrop for fantasy. Fantasy writer N. K. Jemisin's book *The Killing Moon* delves into the lives of high priests inspired by Egyptian society. In the book, the priests of the dream goddess harvest dreams and guide dreamers into the afterlife.

Egyptian Stargazing

Egyptian astronomy spread throughout Africa due in part to the Egyptians' expansive trade routes, which crossed into the Horn of Africa and south of the Sahara. Manuscripts from Timbuktu in West Africa reference the Egyptian reach, and astrological understanding is nearly omnipresent in art and architecture from the region.

Lore aside, it's a fact that the Great Pyramid of Giza and others have a host of sky-bound connections. Pyramids were arranged to align with the movement of constellations, solstice sunrises, and cardinal points on the compass. The star Sirius was associated with the annual flooding of the Nile River. Egyptians had a very sophisticated understanding of astronomy that permeated everyday life.

Ancient Nubian culture has a symbiotic relationship with Egypt. The two often shared pharaohs, deities, and history. The two are sister cultures in many ways. Nubia may predate Egypt. Nestled in modern-day Sudan, just south of modern Egypt, Nubia was also known for its stellar architecture and rich cosmology. Unfortunately, the building of the Aswan Dam some decades ago flooded many ancient Nubian sites and ruins. Much of it is currently covered by water.

Symbolically, Egypt and Nubia predate and rival the Western world's anchor in ancient Greece and Rome.

The Dogon

The Dogon have perplexed Western scholars for centuries. Some believe that this Mali-born ethnic group, with an astronomical lore that goes back three millennia, harbors the ancient wisdom of the Egyptians. The stories of the Dogon opened the floodgate of alternative histories and tales inspired by probable outer-space human origins.

According to the Dogon cosmology, the Sirius system is the home to the Nommos, a race of amphibians akin to mermaids and mermen who visited Earth thousands of years ago. They arrived on Earth in an ark—inspiring Perry's Black Ark and Clinton's mothership myths—and imparted the wisdom of the stars.

French anthropologists Marcel Griaule and Germaine Dieterlen conducted and recorded conversations with Dogon priests between the 1930s and '50s because they were dumbfounded by the Dogon's common star knowledge, all assessed without a telescope. The Dogon knew that the star Sirius has two companion stars, the Digitaria (*po tolo*) and Sorghum (*emme ya tolo*). They knew that Digitaria has a fifty-year orbit cycle, and they were also familiar with the rings of Saturn and Jupiter's moon. Robert K. G. Temple's book *The Sirius Mystery* was published in 1977 and popularized these Dogon myths and knowledge.

Scientists would later challenge Griaule and Dieterlen's findings as well as Temple's extraterrestrial leanings, arguing that there's no way this culture—without conventional astronomical technology—could possibly know about star orbits and distant moons. And yet the Dogon have conducted ceremonies since, and have art depicting their knowledge from, as early as the thirteenth century.

The brightest star in the night sky, Sirius is a popular star in legend and lore, with mentions in the *Iliad*, *Star Trek*, and *Men in Black*. But no story rivals the creation story of the Dogon.

Artist Cauleen Smith says she is fixated with the Dogon and used their theme in her 2012 show at the Museum of Contemporary Art in Chicago. "I spent a few days in the astronomy research center reading about the star Sirius. [Scientists] will spend a whole chapter on how it's impossible for the Dogon to know about this star. They are even willing to consider that aliens from outer space told them," she says. "Why do they have a seven-hundred-year-old ritual for a star that they cannot see?"

The Dogon astronomy is held by many Afrofuturists as proof of the advanced science minds and talents of the ancient world. "It represents an African source," says Akpem, who teaches about the star's creative inspirations in her college-level Afrofuturism course. "It represents a cosmology that predates Western discoveries," she continues. Afrofuturist bloggers from the AfrofuturistAffair.com to FuturisticallyAncient.com and Black ScienceFiction.com have posted essays and YouTube videos heralding the star. Art and stories relating to the star Sirius as well as galactic-origin metaphors are attributed to the Dogon.

African Mermaids and Mami Wata

Dogon lore is also one of the sources of the Mami Wata and African mermaid myths. Mami Wata are the pantheon of African water deities—half human, half sea creature. Other Mami Wata include the Togo's Densu and Yoruba's Olokun. However, the Dogon say their stories of Nommos, the mermen and mermaids of their ancestors, came from Egyptian stories. "Most were honored and respected as being 'bringers of divine law' and for establishing the theological, moral, social, political, economic, and cultural foundation, to regulating the overflow of the Nile, and regulating the ecology i.e., establishing days for success at sailing and fishing, hunting, planting etc. to punishment by devastating floods when laws and taboos were violated," writes Mama Zogbé, Mamaissii Vivian Hunter-Hindrew, EdM, author of *Mami Wata: Africa's Ancient God/dess Unveiled*.[3]

Even the words Mami and Wata have Egyptian origins. *Ma* or *mama* means "truth and wisdom," and *Wata* comes from the ancient Egyptian word *uati*, meaning "ocean water."

Contemporary images of Mami Wata are mostly women with long hair and snakes circling their torsos. The image was created by a nineteenth-century German artist but was inspired by the ancient imagery of the Egyptian goddess Isis. Isis was also depicted with braided hair and two serpents draped around her neck. (Isis and Mary, mother of Jesus, also are similarly depicted, as a mother holding a child.) According to myth, when she's not sea bound, she walks the streets of modern African cities and has "avatars" that do the same. She gives wealth to her followers.

The Mami Wata are also closely associated with Africans brought to the New World in the transatlantic slave trade. They inspired the Drexciya myth, of female slaves thrown overboard who now live under the sea. Mami Wata are also a favorite of graphic and installation artists, with odes on sites such as MermaidsofColor.tumblr.com.

Aker, blogger for Afrofuturist website FuturisticallyAncient. com, argues that Mami Wata permeate popular black culture. R&B star Aaliyah's slithering snake adornments in the "We Need a Resolution" video and the floating scene in the "Rock the Boat" video are archetypical references to Isis/Mami Wata. Even Tina Turner's rocking "Proud Mary (Rolling on the River)" evokes water goddess lore.

"Originally recorded by Creedence Clearwater Revival, the song was famously covered by Ike and Tina Turner. The name of the band that originally recorded it as well as the lyrics suggests a religious theme. Proud Mary is a 'riverboat queen' and its name reminds me of Virgin Mary, whose name come from Stalla Maris, 'the star of the sea.' Virgin Mary is often syncretized with Mami Wata or Erzulie," writes Aker.[4]

Nona Hendryx and Labelle speckled their sci-fi rock with mermaid tops and tails and fin-like hair. CopperWire's sole woman, Meklit Hadero, has an alias of Ko Ai, a character whose mythology says she is a messenger species that swims through electrical networks and doubles as a mermaid.

Hip-hop starlet Azealia Banks adopts the cosmetic mermaid motif too, adorned with the trademark colorful long hair and shell tops. With her Mermaid Balls and aquababes, the quick-witted lyricist taps into the fantasy ideal, complete with a *Fantasea* mix tape and songs titled "Neptune" and "Atlantis."

Although Banks doesn't credit her water-themed inventions to Mami Wata per se, she says that the basic idea was inspired by an invitation to designer Karl Lagerfeld's house and a need to impress him. "I can't just look like the rap chick," she told *Spin*, so she dyed her hair green, blue, and purple for the appearance. "I looked like a fish," she said. It's telling that the young ingenue's disdain for rap-borne limitations and her desire to break free of stereotypes led her to be redefined as a classic water goddess.[5]

Continent of Stars

In June 2012 the National Museum of African Art, nestled in DC's epic Smithsonian Institution, unveiled a one-of-a-kind exhibit: *African Cosmos: Stellar Arts*. The brainchild of deputy director and chief curator Christine Mullen Kreamer, *African Cosmos* presented the legacy of continental art inspired by the cosmos, which stretches across thousands of years, threading distant cultures and times. Kreamer combined her lifelong fascination with stargazing and her work as a curator to assemble art, both ancient and modern, that spoke to the incredible influence of sky matters on art created by Africans. Heralded for its depth and perspective, the show was a whopping aha moment for spectators and journalists alike, many of whom had never thought about Africa's science-inspired art. "This exhibition, many years in the making, is part of the museum's series focusing on Africa's contributions to the history of knowledge—in this case, knowledge about the heavens and how this knowledge informs the creation of spectacular works of art," said Kreamer.

Works in the exhibit included an ancient Egyptian mummy board with an ornamented image of the sky goddess, Nut; the legendary Dogon sculptures; Yoruba sculptures honoring the thunder deity, Shango, and wind and lightning goddess, Oya; several Bamana antelope crest pieces, whose open-work manes imply the sun's path through the sky; as well the Tabwa and Luba sculptures.

From ancient Nubian art on papyrus to a towering contemporary *Rainbow Serpent* made of repurposed containers, Kreamer's impressive show gave definition to the too often ignored and often undefined legacy of African thoughts on the sky.

The exhibit featured contemporary artists as well, including El Anatsui, the late Alexander "Skunder" Boghossian, Willem Boshoff, Garth Erasmus, Romuald Hazoumè, Gavin Jantjes, William Kentridge, Julie Mehretu, Karel Nel, Marcus Neustetter, and Berco Wilsenach.[6] It was the first major exhibit of its kind.

There's a tendency to view Africa for its cultural contributions in music and art, Kreamer told me, and a reluctance to understand the continent's long-standing contributions to science and our understanding of astronomy.

The African understanding of the universe is highly personal, says Kreamer. And the one hundred works showcased in the exhibit depicted relationships between humanity, the sun, moon, stars, and celestial phenomena. More than religious symbols or decorative art, these works were complex webs of philosophy and science that gave new meaning to life.

Traditionally, African cultures don't separate science and art in the Western perspective of the divide. Dr. Malidoma Patrice Somé was boggled by the difference. "In Western reality, there is a clear split between the spiritual and the material, between religious life and secular life. This concept is alien to the Dagara," writes Somé.[7] Cultural astronomy, according to Kreamer, is the study of "lay experts and nonexperts who relate in the broadest sense to the sky," and it gives a language to the non-Western ideals of bridging science, art, and wisdom. Although cultural astronomers focus heavily on native cultures in North and South America, Africa, says Kreamer, is ripe for rigorous study.

"In contrast to the Western inclination to separate bodies of knowledge into distinctive fields, African systems are often more expansive and inclusive, bringing together philosophical, religious and scientific concepts into a more holistic approach toward comprehending reality," Kreamer writes in her book *African Cosmos,* a companion piece to the exhibit. Kreamer, among others, argues that the failure to view African art and science from an African perspective creates a gaping hole in the global knowledge base.

When I called Kreamer to interview her for this book, she initially didn't quite understand how her show fit into a conversation about Afrofuturism. I shared that many Afrofuturists incorporate African mythology and spirituality in their work. The *African Cosmos* exhibit is a reminder that there is a legacy of weaving art, philosophy, and the realms of the sky from a black and African perspective that predates the term Afrofuturism and any newfound curiosity. A life inspired by science fiction resides in the myths and art of the ages.

"Afrofuturism has always been a part of our culture," award-winning filmmaker Wanuri Kahiu said at TEDx Nairobi. Kahiu said that many African myths and folktales are laced with spiritualism and science fiction. "It's always been a part of us," she said.

This connection to an African and African-diasporic perspective and other ancient wisdom is one that Afrofuturists seek.

A Cultural Astronomer

Dr. Jarita Holbrook dedicates her life to uncovering the history of African stargazing. "My work as a researcher fills in the blanks. When you say African astronomy, there are only two [cultures] that come to mind, the Egyptians and the Dogon. The point was to give a voice to everyone else," she says.

In fact, the spark for the study of cultural astronomy in sub-Saharan African is credited to the study of the Great Zimbabwean ruins in the nineteenth century that were found to align with celestial bodies. The Igbo, Bamana, Sandawe, Yoruba, Fante, and many others have rich astronomy cultures as well, and anthropologists and others are dedicated to their unearthing and documentation.

Holbrook studied a host of African cultures and their traditional relationships to the sky, and she is a big advocate for recognizing black astrophysicists. When asked how her curiosity in African cultural astronomy was piqued, she gives a one-word answer: "Racism." Trained in astrophysics, Holbrook grew annoyed with the stares and odd questions she received as she studied for her PhD. "There's a weird hazing. [People] act as if you don't belong," says Holbrook, who is also researching the trajectory of black women with PhDs in astrophysics and documenting the writing scripts in Africa with Kreamer. "But there is a history of black people looking at the sky."

In fact, at the time of our interview, she was crowd-sourcing funds to shoot the documentary *Black Sun*, which follows two African American astrophysicists traveling to Australia and Japan to monitor the solar eclipse. When she's not researching or teaching cultural astronomy, Holbrook's writing science fiction. The Astronaut Tribe series, a yet-to-be-published work, is her debut sci-fi venture and was recently optioned for a film.

Holbrook began her career in African cultural astronomy by studying coastal groups and how they currently use the stars for navigation. She looked at sites in Tunisia in North Africa as well as Tanzania and Eritrea to the east and Gambia and Ghana in the west. Using the stars to navigate is a common practice, she says, adding, "I believe that, pretty much, you can walk around the coast of Africa and you can find people who navigate by the stars."

She continues, "I'm very interested in women's relationship to the sky and how they often use the moon to regulate their fertility." She notes that the book *Blood Magic*, edited by Thomas Buckley and Alma Gottlieb, points to African groups that look to the moon to determine where they are on their cycles. The planet Venus is connected with a feminine deity in African societies too. Holbrook says, "In West Africa, they tie the women initiation ceremony for the Mande family with Venus. Before the ceremony, they watch Venus to determine when the ceremony should begin."

In 2006 Holbrook organized the first international conference on African cultural astronomy. The weeklong event was set to coincide with the solar eclipse on March 29 and brought the world's African cultural astronomers together. Two years later she coedited *African Cultural Astronomy* with scholars R. Thebe Medupe and Johnson O. Urama, including essays on recent findings, research, and the conference itself. This body of work was a groundbreaking effort to bolster the study of African cultural astronomy and to integrate it into schools and universities. Research spanned the continent, looking to literature, art, lore, and anthropology. Holbrook hopes to catalog all of the cultural anthropological research and myths across the continent as well as the African scripts with sky symbols.

However, much of what scholars know about African cultural astronomy comes from African art. This was one of the reasons Holbrook was excited about the "African Cosmos" show. She says, "If they put their art on a semipermanent medium like the cast iron of the Dahomey—or wood carvings, stone carvings—those that practice in that medium can survive the times. Certain cultures we don't know [about], because they weren't using materials that would last." Most African cultures have an agricultural calendar that's directed by the sky and a creation story in which either their ancestors or God is connected to the sky, says Holbrook. "They'll have artwork that is connected to the sky. Popular things to depict are the Milky Way, Venus, the sun, and the moon."

Moreover, the animals used to describe groups of constellations reflect the region. "If you look at Pacific Island names for stars, you won't find lions or bears, but you will find stingrays and fish. In Africa, you have giraffes, wildebeest, you have lions, and depending on where you are, you have leopards," she says. She also says that because much of Africa is in the tropics, the constellations are arranged differently and follow tropical archaeoastronomy. "Not only does the sky look different and move differently, if you're in the tropics, the sun, moon, and stars are directly overhead at some point. Outside of the tropics, stars are either south or north. When you live in the tropics, you don't have stars that circle. Those in the tropics all see things move the same way."

Holbrook also works with the Timbuktu Astronomy Project, helmed by Medupe. "We're looking at the translation of Muslim astronomy in Africa," she says. Medupe looks for variations in mathematics and science in the Arabic texts in various regions to determine if the local Africans modified it.

However, Holbrook doesn't believe that Africa is unique in its historical and cultural relationship with the sky. "These things are common for cultures in Africa and are common for cultures in the world," she adds. "The nature of racism is one where they expect Africans to have done nothing. So when you imply that they did things, or did what everyone else did, it's earth-shaking. Why would Africans look at the sky? Why wouldn't they? I feel like I have this activist role. Here I am causing trouble, finding that Africans study the sky." Although the Egyptians and Dogon are highly researched, she encourages Afrofuturists to explore the plethora of African cultural astronomy, although she admits that information can be hard to come by. Nevertheless, the Somali, Mande (to which the Dogon belong), Dahomey, and Igbo are among those with intriguing cosmologies too, she says. "There's so much work to be done," she adds.

Umberto Eco wrote that writers are inspired by a question and their book is the answer. This simple insight into the nature of creativity applies to Afrofuturists as well. The mythmaking and time-travel themes and celebration of ancient wisdom are steam-powered by this idea that there simply must be more to the mythological canon than the stories we inherit. Just as Greek, Roman, and Norse myths undergird Western art, literature, entertainment, and architecture, Afrofuturists are among those thirsty for other ancient frameworks.

The mythology and beliefs that shaped African societies in antiquity are the greatest mystery of them all. Much of the records of these societies were purposely destroyed by invading societies. The dam built over Nubian homelands and ruins and Napoleon's destruction of the historic library in Alexandria are just the tip of the iceberg. When ancient Egyptian language was banned following the nation's takeover by Rome and later the Arabs, even the translation of the hieroglyphics was lost to the world, only to be restored centuries later by the painstaking work of linguists. But Egypt and Nubia withstood the test of time. Many ancient societies that thrived in the past are lost to us forever. If they were lucky, their art survived the perils of time. How many other wisdom traditions vanished in the rubble of history? What stories and heroes are lost in the winds of time? And what, if anything, could such tales from cultures past inform us of today about our humanity, our origins, and the purpose of life? How could this distant wisdom enrich our lives today?

I sometimes feel that Afrofuturism is the subconscious's way of knocking at the door of present awareness, infusing those who are receptive with ideas and stories from worlds and times forever lost. Perhaps the mythmaking of today is the legacy and the subconscious, just the goddess's way of sharing a vision.

THE DIVINE FEMININE IN SPACE

D r. Mae Jemison, the first black woman to go into space, always liked math and technology. But her space dreams were sparked by watching Lieutenant Uhura, the lone black character on *Star Trek*, each week. The role of Uhura, played by Nichelle Nichols in the 1960s, has been reprised by Zoe Saldana in recent years. Nichols was one of the only black women on television in the 1960s and, next to Diahann Carroll's Julia, one of the few who weren't playing maids.

Uhura was written into *Star Trek* in part to use the show as a commentary about racial equality. But Nichols was frustrated that her character's story line was underutilized, and she submitted a letter of resignation. The story goes that civil rights leader Dr. Martin Luther King Jr. hoped to change her mind.

"He said, 'I'm the biggest Trekkie on the planet and I am Lieutenant Uhura's most ardent fan,'" Nichols recalled. "'You can't abdicate your position,' he said. 'You are changing the minds of people across the world. For the first time, through you, we see ourselves. What we can be, what we are fighting for, what we are marching for.'" Nichols was convinced.[1]

In 2012 Mae Jemison launched the 100 Year Starship project, a nonprofit whose goal is to achieve interstellar travel by 2112.

And it all began with a fictitious character.

Mythmaking

"Women have a different approach in the way that they use Afrofuturism," says art curator Ingrid LaFleur.

On November 11, 2011 (11-11-11), LaFleur launched *My Mythos*, an all-female Afrofuturist art show at Pittsburgh's Fe

Gallery. The show featured critically acclaimed artists Ayanah Moor, Alisha Wormsley, Krista Franklin, Staycee Pearl, and D. Denenge Akpem. "*My Mythos* examines how we create personal mythologies as a vehicle for transformation in order to achieve a new truth," writes LaFleur. The artists, she adds, are "visionaries guiding our consciousness into their imagined realities."

Most mythical creations are borrowed from ancient stories, but in Afrofuturism, artists are encouraged to create their own. Franklin, a poet and mixed-media collagist, showcased her series *The Untold Legend of Naima Brown*. Brown is a young shape-shifter who leaves a trail of coiled hair after every transformation. "She's a shape-shifter who could weave hair," says LaFleur. According to the myth, a childhood friend collects the hair, and the works in Franklin's show are made of Brown's remnants.

Wormsley created a story of a postapocalyptic world in which only black women and white men survived. "The men are trying to procreate, and they are in a sterile environment. So these women are in pods, and there's a video that explains the whole story," says LaFleur.

Akpem featured ceiling-draped decor inspired by her ancestors who moved to California for the Gold Rush. "She has these really great golden nuggets that swirl around," says LaFleur. A choreographer, Pearl's multimedia display cast a dancer transitioning from familiar to unfamiliar worlds. Moore, a printmaker, made her first multimedia work, an image of *Ebony* magazine that moved along a scanner. "She left it up to us to create our own mythology," says LaFleur.

Afrofuturism is a free space for women, a door ajar, arms wide open, a literal and figurative space for black women to be themselves. They can dig behind the societal reminders of blackness and womanhood to express a deeper identity and then use this discovery to define blackness, womanhood, or any other identifier in whatever form their imagination allows.

Afrofuturists are not the first women to do this. Fine artist Elizabeth Catlett, author Zora Neale Hurston, and anthropologist/choreographer Katherine Dunham, among others, used imagination, art, and technology to redefine black and female expressions. However, Afrofuturism as a movement itself may be the first in which black women creators are credited for the power of their imaginations and are equally represented as the face of the future and the shapers of the future. Afrofuturism celebrates women like Catlett, Hurston, and Dunham for using the imagination as a space of resistance and establishes a lineage of this history of thought.

In Afrofuturism, black women's imagination, image, and voice are not framed by the pop expectations and sensibilities of the day. The black woman is not held to Middle America's norms, trying to prove that she's not government dependent or aspiring to the beauty ideals in the latest blogs. Nor is there some uniform expectation of blackness that she is called to maintain. Women develop theories, characters, art, and beauty free of the pressures of meeting male approval, societal standards, color-based taxonomies, or run-of-the-mill female expectations. The results are works that some critics call uncategorizable.

While the work is uncategorizable, so too are the creators. Janelle Monáe's song "Q.U.E.E.N." featuring Erykah Badu questions the concept of being a freak or exuding a natural, self-sustaining independence that doesn't fit neatly into society's modest expectations about women of color. They defy acceptable behavior particularly regarding dancing and appearance, with free-form dancing and eccentric dress interpreted as sexual, provocative, and largely unsettling. I'm reminded of a dance performance by A'Keitha Carey at a recent black existentialism conference. Carey, who is exploring Afrofuturism in dance, performed her dance style, CaribFunk, a fusion of classical ballet, modern, pilates fitness, and Afro-Carribean dance styles. The performance highlighted hip rotations, akin to belly dancing, and fluid arm movements. Let me note that the performance was not designed to tease sexually or stir up any sensuous emotions. After presenting, one curious male observer asked her how does one look at such a performance and not think about sexuality? How does one not objectify the performer? The very presence of a woman in control of her body was unsettling and for some triggered instant objectification. "They call us dirty because we break all your rules down," Monáe sings in "Q.U.E.E.N." "Even it makes others uncomfortable, I wanna love who I am."

Magic Is Real

Many Afrofuturist authors are described as sci-fi and Afro-surrealist, magical realist and fantasy, simply because their work links science, nature, and magic as one. It's a thin line to walk.

L. A. Banks wrote the *Vampire Huntress* series. Although her work is technically horror and follows a young woman coming of age, the multiculturalism, historical context of African and South American cultures, and the earth-based magic had her writing beyond genre. Toni Morrison is known for mixing hauntings and spirituality, too. Neither woman used Afrofuturism as her paradigm, but this world-crossing quest where the visible is as alive as the invisible punctuates art by black women. Artist/ professors John Jennings and Stanford Carpenter call this presence of ghost stories and hauntings in black literature and art the "ethno-gothic" and believes it's a way of dealing with cultural trauma. But the expression of mysticism and nature is reminiscent of the divine feminine recognized in faiths across the world.

In general, Afrofuturism is a home for the divine feminine principle, a Mother Earth ideal that values nature, creativity, receptivity, mysticism, intuition, and healing as partners to technology, science, and achievement. The divine feminine is the other side to the information-gathering process, and tapping into it is a process of choice for many Afrofuturists. There's a widespread belief that humankind has lost a connection to nature, to the stars, to a cosmic sense of self, and that reclaiming the virtues of the divine feminine will lead to wholeness. Many men in the genre embrace the principle as much as the women do.

In film, the idea of a divine feminine is best represented by the Oracle in the *Matrix* trilogy. Played by Gloria Foster in the first two films and Mary Alice in the third, the Oracle is Neo's guide to understanding himself. But rather than giving clear-cut advice, the Oracle is more likely to give Neo thoughts to ponder, and he must make sense of her wisdom with his power of choice.

"You've already made the choice," she tells Neo. "Now you have to understand it."[2]

Valuing the divine feminine is one way that Afrofuturism differs from sci-fi and the futurist movements in the past. In Afrofuturism, technological achievement alone is not enough to create a free-thinking future. A well-crafted relationship with nature is intrinsic to a balanced future too.

The feminine aspect of humanity reigns freely in Afrofuturism. The subconscious and intuition, which metaphysical studies dub as the feminine side of us all, are prioritized in the genre. This feminine side is neither guided by Western mythology nor limited by popular takes on history. Women Afrofuturists have decision-making power over their creative voice. They make their own standards and sculpt their own lens through which to view the world and for the world to view them. Most important, their voice is not specifically shaped in opposition to a male or racist perspective. While Afrofuturist women are obviously shaped by modern gender issues, their creations and theories themselves emerge from a space that renders such limitations moot. The main commonality is their individuality and a desire to encourage free thinking and end the -isms that have plagued the present and the recent past.

Afrofuturist women get a kick out of rewiring their audiences. The muses and icons that've inspired the genre always appear to have sprung up from nowhere. Grace Jones, Octavia Butler, Erykah Badu, Janelle Monáe, for example, are just hard to place. Even their personal histories and private lives are shrouded in mystery. On the surface, these women don't fit neatly into any artistic movement or the history of the times without a healthy dose of explanation.

"Am I a freak? Or just another little weirdo? Call me weak, or better yet—you can call me your hero, baby," Janelle Monáe sings in the song "Faster."

"That's what I've always been fighting for," Monáe says, "making sure that people love themselves for who they are, and we don't pick on people because we're uncomfortable with ourselves, or who they are. That's been my message, from when I was young to now. There are lots of young girls out there who are struggling with their identities, afraid of being discriminated against or teased. I take risks and use my imagination so that other people will feel free and take risks. That's my hope."[3]

Read Nnedi Okorafor's book *Who Fears Death*, visit D. Denenge Akpem's performance installation *Alter-Destiny 888* or a dance performance by A'Keitha Carey, and flip through Afua Richardson's comic illustrations, and there's a conscious reorientation process that takes place, almost as if you were dropped into a far-off land. But the land feels familiar, a reality that is soothing for some and unsettling for others. It's as if the artists want you to remember something, and they discuss it in such a matter-of-fact way that you figure you must know. But do you? There's an unconscious game of trying to remember a memory, a time or space when and where these familiar oddities weren't so bizarre. It's the familiarity with the seemingly bizarre that leads to the aha moment. Female Afrofuturists create their own norm, and the rest of the world just tries to catch up.

A Star Is Born

Afrofuturism has a star-is-born quality to it. Either morphing from the head of Zeus or crafted from clay like Wonder Woman or her black sister Nubia, there's just a supernatural quality to engaging in the work. Grace Jones is no exception. Jones is a pop-culture phenom whose bold antics, outlandish personality, and dazzling looks defied all norms. There was absolutely nothing about her that was conventional when she hit the world stage in the late 1970s. She is Josephine Baker post women's lib and the black liberation movement, with a steely, feminine-yet-androgynous look that came to define early '80s style and has resurged in the twenty-first century.

A preacher's daughter born in Jamaica, Jones moved to New York as a child and built on her theater training to make the world her stage. Her rocket was launched in the club scene and fashion houses of New York and Paris, where she bridged the exotic and the futuristic in a shock-and-awe manner that screamed power. She was a muse to Andy Warhol, and while she was popular in the 1970s and '80s, by the twenty-first century—when nouveau pop stars recreated her style—she had juggernauted into legend status.

Jones recorded a couple of disco singles in the mid-1970s and eventually landed a record deal with Island Records in 1977. She went on to record a string of underground dance hits in the late '70s and '80s and continued to make music into the 2000s, most recently in 2008. Although her electronic new-wave sound captured the radical shift in music in the 1970s, she is most popular for her radical fashion and style. "I've always been a rebel," says Jones. "I never do things the way they're supposed to be done. Either I go in the opposite direction or I create a new direction for myself, regardless of what the rules are or what society says."[4]

In a 1985 performance at Paradise Garage, an underground dance club, Jones's body-paint adornments and colorful metal-and-wire costume (both designed and executed by artist Keith Haring) morphed native art ideas into futuristic fashion.

A tall, lithe, brown-skinned woman whose angular features were accented by her square-shaped hairdo, everything Jones did in fashion became iconic decades later. "Models are there to look like mannequins, not like real people. Art and illusion are supposed to be fantasy," she says. Her red-carpet looks were jaw-dropping. Her concerts were scary gender-bending carnivals of role reversals. She sported a flattop and fade, a style many black men would adopt nearly a decade later, when most women were going for big-hair glam looks. She established the shoulder-padded look of the '80s that made a high-fashion comeback in 2010. She sported severely tailored pantsuits just as more women entered the workforce.

Styled almost exclusively by Jean-Paul Goude from the late 1970s until the mid-1980s, everything about Jones's outfits, from nude appearances in body paint to floor-length hooded gowns, has been mimicked by Madonna, Lady Gaga, Rihanna, and others. Her style and aggression, boldness and otherworldly reach, embodied Goude's look of the future. Jones's appearances were—and still are—spectacles. In 2012, at age sixty-four, she performed at Queen Elizabeth's Diamond Jubilee celebration. She twirled a hula hoop around her svelte physique while singing "Slave to the Rhythm" and wearing a black-and-red bodysuit and a giant red headdress.

Jones redefined the ideas of beauty, sexuality, and femininity. She wielded fashion as her weapon of choice and inverted beauty standards and women's roles, mesmerizing people in their discomfort. Although she had the help of stylists and producers, Jones has always been Jones.

"But I'm a free spirit," she says. "Where is the wrong? How do I put a limit to freedom?"[5]

Feminist Space

"Afrofuturism is a feminist movement," says Alondra Nelson, Columbia University professor and Afrofuturism theorist who launched the now-legendary Internet Listserv for Afrofuturists. The complex black women characters in black sci-fi stories and the plethora of Afrofuturist women in the arts and beyond are no accident, she says. "There have always been black feminists at the center of the project," she adds.

Many women theorists expanded Afrofuturism's early infatuation with music titans and film to include other arts and social transformation. Sheree R. Thomas, editor of *Dark Matter: A Century of Speculative Fiction from the African Diaspora*, assembled the first major collection of African American science fiction, even including a short story by W. E. B Du Bois. University of Southern California professor Anna Everett organized the early AfroGEEKS conferences that tackled the potential use of the Internet for social change and transformation. And Professor Kara Keeling forged groundbreaking queer-studies research through Afrofuturism.

But claiming a space as feminist doesn't mean it's for women only. What makes a feminist space? "One characteristic is the empowerment of women to work and make decisions in an egalitarian environment," says feminist Jennie Ruby. "Another is the acceptance of women's bodies in all shapes, ages, sizes, and abilities." She continues that, in a feminist space, there's a democracy, a sharing of the workload, and a goal of "valuing nurturance and cooperation over aggression and competition, and working against sexism, racism, heterosexism, ageism, and classism."[6]

"[Afrofuturism] is not a space that women are finding identity; it is a feminist space," Nelson affirms. "Of course it's a space for women to feel empowered, because it's a way to critique the ways people associate with science and technology. I think technology inherently opens the space for women to be central figures in that."

Just as contributions from African descendants to the world's knowledge are frequently viewed as cultural, rather than scientific, the same can be said when looking at the contributions of black women, says Nelson. She points to Madam C. J. Walker, who is widely known as being the first self-made woman millionaire in the US, though she was never hailed as an inventor for creating the products that launched her hair-care empire.

"If Afrofuturism is Africana or black people and engagement and invention around imagination around science and technology, then Madam C. J. Walker fits squarely. The work she was doing was chemistry. It's a kind of technology that was at the prowess of her as a businessperson," says Nelson.

Butler's Renaissance

Octavia Butler is the third point in the Afrofuturism trinity (Sun Ra and George Clinton are the others). Although Harlem-born sci-fi writer Samuel Delany was the first widely recognized black sci-fi writer, Butler struck a special chord with women. "As much as there is an Afrofuturism lineage that comes from Sun Ra, there's one that comes from Octavia Butler," says Nelson.

In a hypermale sci-fi space where science and technology dominate, Butler provided a blueprint for how women, particularly women of color, could operate in these skewed realities and distant worlds. Butler set the stage for multidimensional black women in complex worlds both past and present, women who are vulnerable in their victories and valiant in their risky charge to enlighten humanity.

Butler is known as a sci-fi writer, but like author Nalo Hopkinson, she includes magical surrealism, or seeming magic, in her chosen realities. Moreover, Butler's religious metaphors, central feminine narratives, use of African diasporic mysticism, and the transformative power of love are tenets that many Afrofuturists weave into their work. She gave many women a voice and validated their mashed-up mix of women's issues, race, sci-fi, mysticism, and the future.

"She blew my mind," says award-winning sci-fi writer Nnedi Okorafor, who is amongst Butler's biggest fans. "I was writing these things, and I didn't realize that what I was writing could be published until after I read her work." Okorafor is author of several books, including *Zahrah the Windseeker* and *Who Fears Death*. Both books have hero lead characters with mystical abilities.

"Octavia Butler in her own way served as a role model," says speculative fiction writer N. K. Jemisin. "The [sci-fi] genre itself sends a very clear message that you are not welcome here. I know that every black female writer felt, 'Oh, here's someone like me, and it's OK for us to be here.' Without that moment of validation, that it's OK to be here, I don't know if you'd have as many black women writing in this arena," says Jemisin, who estimates there are at least fifty established black women sci-fi and fantasy writers who are published.

Jemisin was writing sci-fi and fantasy when she was a child. But she didn't write black or women lead characters until she stumbled across Octavia Butler as a teen. "While reading, I said, 'Holy crap, I think this woman is black.' I looked for a photo, and there was none. Instead the book's cover was plastered with the image of a white woman." Photo aside, it was a lightbulb moment for Jemisin. "I had never seen that in sci-fi before," she says. She never thought her lead could be anything other than a white man.

Jemisin's debut novel, *The Hundred Thousand Kingdoms*, was nominated for a Nebula Award, Hugo Award, and the World Fantasy Award. Her follow-up series, *The Killing Moon*, traces the journey and politics of priests in a society reminiscent of ancient Egypt.

There are more women images in science fiction, thanks to Butler and writers like Tananarive Due and Nalo Hopkinson, and the emergence of female sci-fi writers is changing the dynamics of women characters in sci-fi and fantasy. In general, Jemisin feels there's more fascination with the female physique and function than the woman as a whole in most science fiction. She says, "It's a woman through the male gaze—what a woman has to look like to be interesting to men. But it's not as common as it used to be."

Butler herself is often described as a writer's writer. Born in 1948 and reared in sunny Pasadena, California, she says she was inspired to write at age twelve after she watched a campy sci-fi film and figured that she could do better. She is most known for the formerly titled *Xenogenesis* trilogy, since renamed *Lilith's*

Brood for reissue by Warner, the novel *Kindred*, and her *Parable* series. Her heroines are intriguing, overcoming traumas in new lands as a right of passage of sorts in their own evolution.

Alanna Verrick, the adopted daughter of white missionaries, is the heroine in Butler's *Survivor*, the genesis of her Patternmaster myth. Alanna leaves Earth with her adopted parents in the twentieth century to form an Earth colony on an already inhabited planet where half of the planet's warring indigenous citizens are addicted to a powerful drug. Although the missionaries side with the more human-looking, drug-addicted inhabitants, Alanna leads the opposing rebel crew, overcomes addiction, and guides them to a better place in a style reminiscent of the biblical Moses. Her incredible diplomacy, love, and sacrifice win respect.

In *Wild Seed*, Anyanwu, a West African healer with shape-shifting abilities, wrestles with love, desire, and fate through a tortuous bond with the immortal Doru. The twisted relationship sends them through the Middle Passage to Slave States America. Anyanwu, on a quest to create gifted lineage, moves through time and space operating as both man and woman to father and mother ingenious offspring. At one point, she morphs into a dolphin.

Many Afrofuturist writers and artists credit their complex story lines and the popularity of women heroines in Afrofuturist novels and art to Butler's influence with writers, filmmakers, and artists. They point to Butler's quintessential writing as both benchmark and inspiration. Celebrated choreographer and performance artist Staycee Pearl staged *Octavia*, a dance project that dissects Butler's work and life story. Nicole Mitchell composed a symphony to accompany Butler's work, and artist Krista Franklin makes art that depicts Butler's stories. The Carl Brandon Society, an organization dedicated to increasing the representation of people of color in fantastical genres, offers an Octavia E. Butler Memorial Scholarship. Moreover, Spelman College, a college in Atlanta for black women, hosted the Octavia E. Butler Celebration of the Fantastic Arts.

Windseeker

Nnedi Okorafor won the World Fantasy Award in 2011 for her novel *Who Fears Death*. The story follows a black woman in postapocalyptic Africa who studies under a mystical shaman to discover powers that can end the genocide of her people. The child of a brutal attack, her sandy color raises the ire and curiosity of all who see her. Her name is Onyesonwu, which means "who fears death."

Like many Afrofuturist authors, and Butler, before her, Okorafor has a tendency to write beyond the tropes of genre. Her book has been described as magical surrealist, fantasy, and sci-fi. Okorafor says, "There's shamanism, there's juju in it, there's magic, genocide, female circumcision. It deals with issues of African men and women. I based my juju on actual Ebo traditional beliefs. It pulls on the fantastical too."

Okorafor, a Nigerian immigrant to the United States and professor at Chicago State University, writes characters who are outsiders that straddle two worlds. Her books are also pointed cultural critiques. Her depiction of female circumcision, a controversial procedure, drew criticism from several African academics. She named her main character in *Zahrah the Windseeker* Dada,

which means "a child born with naturally (dread)locked hair."
"Before colonialism, that was very special. But after colonialism,
it was considered evil," she says. And her flagrant use of the term
had some calling Okorafor a witch. She says, "My fourth book
was titled *Akata Witch*. It's a derogatory term for African Americans or American-born Nigerians. *Akata* means 'bush animal.'
It's not a very nice term. The book deals with those issues too."

Collective memory and trauma is an issue that concerns
some Afrofuturists, and many women artists and writers use the
aesthetic as a healing device. D. Denenge Akpem, who teaches
Afrofuturism as a pathway for liberation, studies how ritual healing in art can heal trauma, particularly in women. Her performance installation *Alter-Destiny 888* was one of her foray's into
the possibilities of Afrofuturism as ritual. The show opened on
August 8, 2008 (8-8-8), at the Roger Smith Hotel in New York. For
ten days, Akpem performed a self-created ritual of song, including the creation and destruction of clay babies, the building of
an elaborate headpiece in honor of the trickster god Pan, and
the mashing of remaining clay to dust. "The piece was based on
the concept of the alter destiny and of transformation that Sun
Ra addressed," Akpem told Tempestt Hazel, curator/cofounder of
Sixty Inches From Center: The Chicago Arts Archive and Collective Project. "But it was personalized in the sense that I focused
primarily on the question of whether one does have the power to
alter one's destiny and whether one might act as conduit to affect
global destiny or to heal trauma in collective cellular and psychic
memory," she said, noting that women hide their trauma.[7]

She continued, "What alternate destinies were set in motion
through this performance-installation, I am honestly not sure.

What I do know is that the intention was there; the manifestation occurred."

Butler may have inspired black women in sci-fi, and Delany, a sci-fi titan we'll discuss later, helped shape the literary canon of the twentieth century, but African American sci-fi and speculative fiction began long before either of them was born.

W. E. B. Du Bois is an American icon. He is known for countless achievements that shifted race dynamics in America: he was one of the quintessential proponents of civil rights in the early twentieth century, he was amongst the founders of the NAACP, he was a proponent of higher education among blacks, he was one of the early black-history documentarians and founded a sociology department at Atlanta University, he was a Pan-Africanist. Du Bois's theories defined turn-of-the-century strategies on race. His dueling views with Tuskegee University founder Booker T. Washington are classic. Both men, we've discovered, were right. Du Bois's essays on double consciousness and the Talented Tenth are still hot topics in the new millennium.

But few know that Du Bois was also a science fiction writer.

"The Comet," a short story that first appeared in a 1920 collection titled *Darkwater: Voices from Within the Veil*, is Du Bois's primary sci-fi work. The story follows Jim Davis, a black man who quietly resents the nation's skin games. He's sent into a dangerous underground vault to retrieve records—a task no white man would do, he dutifully notes. During his subterranean quest, a mysterious comet hits, and Davis is the last man standing. But he quickly grows comfortable with his ill-timed fate, dining in a whites-only restaurant and driving his own car. Suddenly the freedom that escaped him in daily life is at his fingertips. Clearly, this disaster has some advantages. He meets a young white woman who was also saved in the peril. Although she initially can't see Davis past her bias and views his brown skin as alien, she moves past prejudice and falls for him. The responsibility of repopulating Earth consumes her passion. Just as the two are about to consummate their love, they are discovered by a rescue team. To Davis's dismay, the comet destroyed New York, but the rest of the world is the same. The woman returns to her wealthy husband, and Davis remains at the bottom of the status quo.[1]

In Du Bois's analogy, race imbalances were so entrenched that only a catastrophe could bring equity. What is a catastrophe for most of the city—a town ravaged by death and destruction—is a fresh new start with thwarted hopes of self-expression and prosperity for Davis and people of color.

I'm not surprised that Du Bois would write a sci-fi story. As a man who devised strategies for eradicating race imbalances for much of his life and who staunchly believed that intellectual achievement could bring political parity, sci-fi was both a great release and the ideal tool to ponder the what-ifs in climbing through a rigid race-based social structure. He placed a thoughtful black man at the heart of his story and displayed the frailties and dilemmas of hope in a world resistant to change. As a fervent activist, Du Bois pushed for many social changes, most of which blossomed after his lifetime. With the tug and pull of a transitioning landscape at the turn of the century—the hope of the end of slavery, the horror at the institution of Jim Crow and mob lynchings, the progression of a small upper class, and the undermining of the larger masses—I wonder if Du Bois, too, felt like he was seesawing between progress and devolution.

However, Du Bois was one of many activists who, beginning in the nineteenth century, used speculative fiction and sci-fi to hash out ideas about race, re-create futures with black societies, and make poignant commentary about the times. We don't know how many black speculative writers were published in the late nineteenth century. The dime novels and pulp magazines of the day didn't reveal the race of their writers, and it was assumed they were white.

"I believe I first heard Harlan Ellison make the point that we know of dozens upon dozens of early pulp writers only as names: They conducted their careers entirely by mail—in a field and during an era when pen-names were the rule rather than the exception," writes Samuel Delany, one of the first major African American science fiction writers of the twentieth century. "Among the 'Remmington C. Scotts' and the 'Frank P. Joneses' who litter the contents pages of the early pulps, we simply have no way of knowing if one, three, or seven of them—or even many more—were not blacks, Hispanics, women, native Americans, Asians, or whatever. Writing is like that."[2]

However, a number of short stories and articles have surfaced, most written by well-meaning activists who, for fleeting moments, turned to speculative fiction to articulate their frustrations and hopes for the future. Martin Delany, for example, was born in West Virginia to a free mother and slave father in 1812. He became one of the first African Americans to attend Harvard Medical School and was the first African American field officer in the Civil War. It was allegedly his proposition and not that of colleague Frederick Douglass that convinced Lincoln to use black soldiers in the war. Delany helped Douglass and William Lloyd Garrison launch the *North Star* newspaper, one of the leading abolitionist papers of the era, in the 1840s. An abolitionist himself, Delany worked with escaped slaves and adopted early black nationalistic beliefs, later doing some work to acquire land in Liberia.

However, Delany was a writer as well. Shortly after the slave insurrection panics of 1856 and the *Dred Scott* decision of

1857—which declared that blacks were not citizens of any state— and a year shy of the war that would split the nation in two, Delany released *Blake: or, the Huts of America*, a speculative fiction serial. The story follows Henry Blake, a revolutionary who convinces blacks in the United States to rise up and found a black nation in Cuba. The story was partially published in the *Anglo American* in 1859 and republished in the *Weekly Anglo American* from 1861 to 1862.[3] *Blake* was published as a book in 1970.

Social activist and Baptist minister Sutton E. Griggs was born in Chatfield, Texas, in 1872. He published more than thirty-three books encouraging African American solidarity and pride. But his best-known work is the controversial *Imperium in Imperio*. Published in 1899, the book is a response to Edward Bellamy's utopian *Looking Backward* and a criticism of its handling of race. *Imperium in Imperio* follows African American friends Belton Piedmont and Bernard Belgrave, both of whom graduate from college. Bernard is elected congressman, and Belton heads to a black college in Louisiana, only to be lynched. Belton survives the lynching, kills the doctor who tries to vivisect him, and wins in court due to Bernard's stellar defense. Belton invites Bernard to join the Imperium in Imperio, a secret African American government in Waco, Texas. Belton wants assimilation; Bernard wants revolution. Bernard's plan to take over Texas and make it an African American nation state is approved by the society, and Belton is executed by the Imperium.

New York lawyer and educator Edward A. Johnson also was inspired by *Looking Backward* and wrote the book *Light Ahead for the Negro* in 1904. A work of utopian speculative fiction, Johnson's book depicts an African American at the turn of the twentieth century who visits America in 2006. Blacks in the South can read, and the coveted forty acres and a mule have finally been distributed. The book shows how the post-racial world evolved over the century. A decade later, in 1917, Bellamy was elected the first African American to serve in the New York State legislature.

Francis E. W. Harper was a social reformer, feminist, and one of the most popular poets of her time. Her book *Iola Leroy*, published in 1892, takes place against a feminist backdrop in which the races are unequal. Iola, the main character of the story, is a pro-slavery Southern belle who learns that her mother was a slave of mixed heritage, therefore meaning that Iola, too, is a slave. "The rest of the novel captures her adventures, and concludes with the establishment of Harper's version of the 'ideal polity'—women active as doctors and activists, large schools taught by married women, and an area in which former slaves can live peacefully and productively. In the context of 1892 and Reconstruction South, this image was indeed a fantastic utopia," writes author and librarian Jess Nevins.[4]

In 1902 Pauline Hopkins, one of the most influential black editors of the early twentieth century, wrote *Of One Blood*, a book that was serialized in the *Colored American*. Protagonist Reuel Briggs, who has little interest in African American history, travels to Ethiopia on an archaeological expedition and discovers the ancient city of Telessar, inhabited by the descendants of the Ethiopia of 6000 BCE and owners of advanced crystal-based technology and telepathy technology.

George S. Schuyler was a Rhode Island–born journalist who both criticized organized religion and was known for more conservative views. He was not a fan of most literature from the Harlem

Renaissance nor was he an admirer of Du Bois. His book *Black No More* profiles a scientist who discovers how to turn black people white. The satire includes a horrid description of the lynching of the money-grubbing inventors by a crowd of whites that painstakingly recreates the gruesome lynchings of black men in the South. In his series "Black Internationale" and "Black Empire," published in the *Pittsburgh Courier* between 1936 and 1938, is the story of Carl Slater, a journalist for the fictional *Harlem Blade* who covers a global battle between white people and people of color. A wealthy intellect leads the battle, gathering top minds in the black diaspora who are frustrated with inequality. The brilliant collective, called Black Internationale, brings the United States to its knees with biological warfare, liberates Africa from its colonizers, and launches air raids that crush Europe. A young, white, female stockbroker aids the movement and becomes head of the European espionage unit.[5]

The idea of using sci-fi and speculative fiction to spur social change, to reexamine race, and to explore self-expression for people of color, then, is clearly nothing new. The black visionaries of the past who sought to alleviate the debilitating system and end the racial divide used these genres as devices to articulate their issues and visions.

This tradition continued with Samuel Delany, Octavia Butler, and Nalo Hopkinson, all of whom merged issues of race, class, sex, sexuality, culture, and identity to make sense of the changing times. Their worlds included people of color, but the issue of otherness was wrapped in a sci-fi space saga that zapped from shape-shifters to gender benders to alien pods, time travel, and killer bodysuits.

Nalo Hopkinson was born in 1960 in Kingston, Jamaica, to a Jamaican mother and Guyanese father. She has lived throughout the Caribbean and South America with stints in the United States and Canada. One of the foremost speculative fiction writers of modern times, she's edited anthologies and published dozens of books and short stories. Caribbean dialect and culture are entrenched in many of her stories, and she candidly deals with postmodern issues of culture, race, and sex.

Brown Girl in the Ring was her first novel. Published in 1998, the dystopian tale depicts a rebel-led Toronto under siege, and the book was hailed for depicting the Carribean community in Toronto and adeptly writing in dialect. The story combines Carribean mysticism and futuristic medicine and includes a disturbing plot involving organ harvesting. But the terror of the city leads the main character to discover some of the old ways and traditions of her grandmother. The book *Sister Mine* follows formerly conjoined twins Makeda and Abby, daughters of a demigod and a human mother. One has magical powers and the other does not, but the two must reconcile to help find their father who disappeared mysteriously.

Hopkinson's short story "Ganger (Ball Lightning)" is a sci-fi story that almost reads like a dark comedy. Published in the anthology *Dark Matter: A Century of Speculative Fiction from the African Diaspora* in 2000, Hopkinson's story plays off Isaac Asimov's 1940s robot stories. Cleve and Issy are a married couple who don't talk anymore. They buy full-bodied sex suits in hopes of saving their marriage only to have the suits turn on them.[6]

"She's a powerful writer with an imagination that most of us would kill for," says Pulitzer Prize–winning author Junot Díaz. "I have read everything she has written and am in awe of her many gifts. And her protagonists are unforgettable—formidable haunted women drawn with an almost unbearable honesty—seriously, who writes sisters like Nalo? Takes courage to be that true." According to sci-fi scholar Gary K. Wolfe, Nalo's family-centered dramas inspired other writers to go beyond sci-fi norms and build on family relationships, too.[7]

By age twenty-six Samuel Delany had written more than eight sci-fi books and won three Nebula Awards. Algis Budrys, a critic with *Galaxy* magazine, declared that Delany, fresh off the release of *Nova*, was "the best science fiction writer in the world." He is one of the most decorated and best-known science fiction writers in the world, credited with influencing cyberpunk as well as Afrofuturism. Some of his later books include intense sexuality that Delany himself has called pornography. He is an inductee in the Science Fiction Hall of Fame and has won four Nebula Awards and two Hugo awards. He has more than twenty novels to his credit.

However, in his essay "Racism and Science Fiction," Delany questions the desire of science fiction institutions to group him with former students Butler and Hopkinson, noting that outside of their race, their work, backgrounds, ages, and perspectives are drastically different. However, the Harlem-born legend adds that the best way to end the "pre-judging" in science fiction worlds is to encourage more nonwhite readers and writers to participate and discuss issues at conferences. When some 20 percent of the audience is composed of people of color the landscape for writers and readers will change, he writes.

When Delany's essay was published in 2000, Afrofuturism as a defined genre had taken root and cadres of writers were looking to Delany, Butler, Hopkinson, and others as literary hallmarks in a genre that was all too dismissive of diversity. In 1999, the Carl Brandon Society was created to increase diversity in speculative fiction. One of its tenants is to "fantasize for its own sake and as an agent of social change." The society offers an Octavia Butler scholarship, honors accomplished writers, and provides supports for new work. More than a decade later, the diversity of sci-fi work and the creators in fiction has given rise to writers like Nnedi Okorafor and N. K. Jemisin, but there are countless others emerging as well. Words inspire visuals. Afrofuturism's visual aesthetic is a playground for the imagination.

8

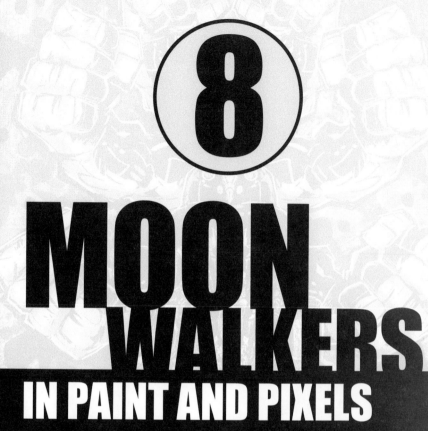

MOON WALKERS

IN PAINT AND PIXELS

mages are powerful. Although the image-making process isn't shrouded in smoke and mirrors like in the old days of Hollywood, and anyone can pull up an editing tutorial on YouTube or watch behind-the-scenes footage on Netflix, the fact remains that most consumers don't process film, videos, photos, paintings, billboards, postcards, and images as a creation by someone else. Viewing images is a pretty passive affair. For many, an image is a statement of fact, even when the image is fictitious.

If I ask you to imagine an alien, chances are that you won't imagine anything. The first wave of images will be flashbacks from movies, comic books, and video games. Whether it's the big, hollow-head ghostlike figure from the alien documentaries or the monstrous humanlike giant in the blockbuster *Prometheus*, it's highly likely that the first pictures to hit your brainwaves will be plucked from popular images in media. I'm placing special emphasis on the word *popular*, because it's the repetition of an image that embeds it in the collective consciousness as a shared emblem.

Images aren't these stand-alone silhouettes. Each comes with a belief system and set of personalized traits. Some of these beliefs are projected by the creator and others are projected by the viewer, but even in this clash, there is a basic consensus, a space where fiction meets some aspect of reality. A drawing of a single smiling fairy can be interpreted as cute, sweet, and sometimes mischievous, in part because the interpretations are based on rehashed stories of the past. But such smiling innocence would never denote the makings of a murderer or the day-to-day work of a stockbroker. There's simply no reference for that association to take place. Fairies aren't killers, and fairies aren't stockbrokers.

Fairies also aren't black. Fairies aren't Latino. Fairies aren't Asian. Fairies aren't men. Fairies aren't overweight. Fairies aren't bald. Despite the fact that stories of fairies can be found throughout the world, from Africa to Southeast Asia, of fairies of different sizes, sexes, hair textures, and personalities, fairies in the larger media world have one uniform look and accepted set of qualities: She's a she, she's petite, she's white. If she doesn't look like Thumbelina or Tinker Bell and can't fit in a size-negative taffeta skirt, she's not a fairy.

Disney wrestled with how to tell a modern story of a black princess, finally putting out *The Princess and the Frog* in 2009. Although I didn't see any official statements saying this, I'd guess that one of the greatest problems when trying to develop the project was that the image of the princess with the sashaying Cinderella hoopskirt and Rapunzelesque hair derived from European folktales is not associated with the image of black women. Although we're talking about a cartoon and playing in the world of fiction, the challenge, I'm sure, was to make the image of a black princess connect with audiences. To make the fantasy work, creators had to work with preconceived images and twentieth-century realities. And yet, there have been black princesses (not as many with hoopskirts and Rapunzelesque hair, of course) in real life since the beginning of time.

Remote Control

Historically, those who fight for equal rights are also fighting for control over their image as well as the development and depiction of their culture. Photos, films, drawings, and visual media at large have both intentionally and unintentionally perpetuated class, sex, and ethnic stereotypes. For decades traditional media and the gallery world were visual-media gatekeepers. If your work didn't filter through their lens of approval, it fought for survival anywhere.

Visual media is the medium of choice for widespread propaganda. *The Birth of a Nation* is recognized for being the first large-scale Hollywood picture, but the story—a propagandist tale of the rise of the Ku Klux Klan during Reconstruction—also embedded the stereotypes of blacks in cinema for nearly a century. The relationship between media, the visual arts, and the dangerous stereotypes so many work to unravel is a serious one. I committed to working in media one day during my junior year in high school when I realized that the books, TV shows, films, and art I soaked in were the only windows to the larger world beyond my day-to-day teen life. Although I was a kid steeped in well-rounded black images, history, and a big heap of positive thinking, not everyone else was.

Images are powerful.

That is why the NAACP, long a forerunner in advocating for diversity in Hollywood, hosts its annual Image Awards show. It's the reason that every time a reality show, film, or sitcom with black characters hits the screen, people debate the merit of the image of blacks in media via message boards, Twitter, and in cafes. It's the reason that, at one point, leaders and fans hoped that hip-hop stars who had the glare of the spotlight upon them might take up the banner for equal rights. It's the reason that art shows are often heralded for untold views of black life. Unfortunately, in the black American experience, images have often been used to frame our lives, how we come to understand ourselves, and how others relate to us. No one's life should be dictated by a flashing photograph or a cartoon.

When DJ Spooky remixed the footage in *The Birth of a Nation*, the music-backed multimedia presentation traveled to museums throughout the world. While many were horrified by the film's depictions, DJ Spooky's exhibit underscored that technology is the ultimate power tool for defining and redefining the image. In the hands of a remixer and with a hint of low-cost editing, the flashing images that had been seared into the nation's lexicon of black stereotypes could be rewound, inverted, chopped, and screwed—or erased. The power of this looming, larger-than-life screen is in the hands of anyone who wants to change it.

Today technology enables a greater ability to create and share images across the world. Social media, websites, music downloads, digital cameras, low-cost sound engineering, at-home studios, editing equipment, and on and on. Upgrades to animation and illustration software happen so quickly that by the time a student is trained on one platform, new illustration software debuts. A decade ago, an up-and-coming kid with an over-the-shoulder video camera needed a heavy light kit, tripod, and reflectors to shoot a good scene. Today they can survive with a near-weightless camera or pop an adjustable lens on a camera phone. Two years ago, a still photographer shot my family reunion photo. A few months ago, a cousin shot the whole bunch (more than a hundred) with her iPad.

Traditional media isn't the information gatekeeper it was in the past. A combination of the Internet, inexpensive digital media, and the proliferation of mobile devices and blogs has allowed artists to create art, write about it, and share their work on a world stage. These artists are bound by a conviction to reshape black images past and present. Meshing the limits of time and space, today's Afrofuturistic artists provide another lens to view the world. While Afrofuturism rippled through a Listserv in the past, today the dialogue has spread through blogs, online newspapers, and Instagram.

A Brand-New World

"People so did not expect a science fiction film out of Africa," *Pumzi* director Wanuri Kahiu told *Bitch* magazine. "Let alone East Africa. People would ask me things like, 'With so many other films to make, why would you make a science fiction film? What does that mean?' Does that mean that because I'm from a certain region, I have a limited capacity of imagination?"[1]

Born and raised in Kenya, Kahiu came to the United States to study film at UCLA and returned to her hometown, Nairobi, to direct films. *Pumzi* is the region's first sci-fi film, and the groundbreaking work picked up awards at festivals across the world. *Pumzi* means "air" in Kiswahili. Raising questions about sustainability and hope, Kahiu provides a never-before-seen image of high-tech Africans in the future.

Pumzi may mark the beginning of a new era in African Afrofuturistic cinema. It's a twenty-one-minute short that follows Asha, an African scientist who lives in the Maitu community, an underground, high-tech futuristic city in East Africa. Some thirty-five years after World War III and the water wars, humans are forced to live underground. Water is rare, and citizens purify their sweat and urine for drinking water. Asha studies soil samples and soon finds one that can bear life. She's awakened by dreams of a sole tree that stands rooted aboveground, but dreaming is so discouraged that when she has one, a talking cyborg instructs her to take a dream suppressant.

Asha is imprisoned for dreaming, and after a friend escapes, she goes aboveground into toxic environments determined to find the source of the life-supporting soil and plant a seed. She ultimately sacrifices herself, using sweat from her body to plant the seed, and in her death, her body provides the nourishment that nurtures the seed into a tree. The images in the film are striking, from the futuristic fashions worn by actress Kudzani Moswela to her bold trek through the sands.

Although the story is pretty straightforward, one critic feared that her own Western feminist sentiments prevented her from understanding the story and writing an insightful critique. Very little about this short was rooted in Western culture, other than the film medium itself, a reality that completely disoriented the writer. Even the universalism of the story and the fact that the lead character was a woman still didn't forge a connection. Was the depiction of tech-savvy futuristic Africans with a desire to connect with nature too different for the writer to analyze? "Maybe I'm Othering Kahiu by equivocating," she concluded, adding that she'd rather the beauty of the film speak for itself.[2]

A Star Is a Seed

"I want to create images no one has seen," said Cauleen Smith, experimental filmmaker and multimedia artist. We were swapping tea in Chicago's Hyde Park, a place now famous for being the home of President Barack Obama, just blocks away from Washington Park and Bronzeville, both of which were Sun Ra's stomping grounds. "It's rare that I see an image in a black film that I want to use or that I think is viable in liberating the imagination," Smith said, noting that the filmmakers from the L.A. Rebellion, a collective of black filmmakers from the UCLA film school, were "masters" of creating the new images that were the antithesis of Hollywood.

Smith has worked as an Afrofuturist artist for twenty years. Like many Afrofuturistic artists, she began working in the aesthetic before Afrofuturism was named. A sci-fi fan, Smith learned how to make experimental films and connected with French structuralist theories, although she didn't like the structuralist aversion to politics.

"I took these structural concepts and merged it with memory and culture. I didn't realize that's what Afrofuturism was—speculating about the past and speculating on the future while reconfiguring the present tense." Smith, at that time a part of a collective called the Carbonist School in Austin, was immediately taken with the idea of blackness as a technology. "We were all into sci-fi," she said, adding, "We came up with this idea that all these artists were using blackness as a technology. It's been used as a technology against us—being marked with a certain race determines your race, your movement, access, and privileges."

She read Greg Tate's work and was intrigued by Samuel Delany, George Clinton, Sun Ra, and other black artists for their use of cognitive estrangement. "Clinton would take all these sci-fi tropes we were familiar with and totally freak it out. But funk was familiar," she said. "The use of cognitive estrangement, shifting perceptions of the images we're all familiar with, that defines the Afrofuturistic artist. . . . Put simply, I would describe Afrofuturism as the experience of cognitive estrangement as manifested through sound, image, language, and form that so often defines or frames the mundane conditions and movements and generative thought in the African diaspora," she recorded in the Chicago Arts Archive. She added, "[Afrofuturism] is not a moniker of identity or geography but a musical, literary, and art-historical movement—like creative music, postmodernism, or conceptual art."[3]

Smith came to Chicago in the summer of 2011 to study Sun Ra's relationship to the city. She's inspired by the relationship between space and art, cities and artists. "Experimentation is very well understood here with the working class. In other cities, the elite class decides that. In Chicago it's the working class who do, and the middle class has to respond. I can see that here."

Digging through the archives at the University of Chicago and interviewing AACM members, Smith wanted to know what role Chicago culture played in Sun Ra's evolution. Her insights were the backdrop for *A Star Is a Seed*, a multimedia show she unveiled at the Museum of Contemporary Art in Chicago in May 2012.

The show was an ode to improvisation as mastery. "You can only improvise when you totally know what you are doing," Smith said. Although other cultures have invoked the beauties of improvisation, Smith believes it was key to the survival of the black diaspora.

A Star Is a Seed was a total challenge to the visual senses. Visitors were first greeted by a collection of old DVD player boxes stacked to the ceiling like blocks. Next attendees saw *The Ark*

After the Flood, a single room featuring video clips from the film *The Secret Life of Plants* projected from a metallic DVD player tilted like the flower on a stem into an aquarium and reflected onto the ceiling. Oddly, *The Secret Life of Plants* is also known for its unique soundtrack by Stevie Wonder, which features a song in tribute to the Dogon's relationship to the star Sirius. In addition to the visual elements, the room also featured variations of the *Wizard of Oz* song "Over the Rainbow" spilling from surround-sound speakers. Played by an array of jazz artists, from Sun Ra to Art Tatum, the song reflects "the fragility and tenuousness of human life, hopes and dreams," Smith said in her artist statement.

A posted statement asked visitors to abandon their notions of time and space as they entered *The Inhfinity Vortex*, a corridor reminiscent of the mirror scene in Bruce Lee's *Enter the Dragon*. Once visitors saw their way through the mass of reflections, they were in a screening room with a bench and two giant fuzzballs fit for sitting. Here, visitors watched a series of short films.

These films featured images Chicagoans would recognize, such as the Bean, officially named *Cloud Gate* at Millennium Park; the lakefront; the cylinder-shaped Hilliard Homes on Twenty-Second and State; and the Statue of the Republic, or Golden Lady, a commemorative relic from the Chicago World's Fair that sits on Sixty-Third Street near Hayes Park. But Smith's depictions of the images maximized her love affair with cognitive estrangement with her verite-style shooting capturing an oddly sci-fi landscape. Even a shot of a manhole on a South Side street suddenly looked like an Egyptian sundial.

There was a film of black kids riding their bikes along the lake, donning glitter capes and bike helmets. There was a shot of the Rich Central Marching Band, a mostly black high school marching band, playing Sun Ra's song "Space Is the Place" in Chinatown. There was a single-shot video of Mwata Bowden, former president of the AACM, playing a six-foot-tall brass instrument that resembled a band of trumpets wrapped together and sounded like a didgeridoo, the popular indigenous instrument commonly played by Australian Aborigines.

Another video featured violinist Renee Baker shocking conventional wisdom by evoking sounds from the violin that were off the chromatic scale. Part percussive, part Jimi Hendrix, part wah-wah pedal, the music she played was fabulous and out of this world. From hypnotizing microphones to toy pyramids, these experimental films were the ultimate in cognitive estrangement, with hometown images morphing into magic emblems and everyday people whipped into musical shamanism. Not a single special effect was used. Oddly, the red-wigged dancing space visitors in one shot, with their Sun Ra quotes written on paper, seemed normal in light of all I'd seen before. Black girls with colorful wigs and bright hairstreaks were part of the fashion of the day.

Space of Resistance

John Jennings is a Jack Kirby fan.

I think it's fair to say that most real comic book fans are Kirby enthusiasts. Kirby, one of the titans in the comic world, is the illustrator and cocreator behind Captain America, the Incredible Hulk, the Avengers, and a host of iconic figures for DC and Marvel Comics. "A lot of Kirby's work was about mythology and heritage," says Jennings, an artist and visual arts professor at SUNY in Rochester. However, Kirby holds a special place in the hearts of many black comic fans because he is also the cocreator of Black Panther, the first black superhero in mainstream American comics.

In tribute to Kirby's foray into black identity and his influence on the comic world, Jennings, along with Stacey "Blackstar" Robinson, created *Black Kirby*, a showcase of a series of candid illustrations recreating classic Kirby covers with an Afrofuturistic motif. "*Black Kirby* is an Afrofuturistic black power fantasy," says Jennings, who says the duo blended Kirbyisms, Afrofuturism, and black pop art to create the show. As creators, he and Robinson took on Jack Kirby's outlook and imagined the kinds of comics he'd have created if he were black. Jennings debuted the show in September 2012 at his alma mater, Jackson State University.

The visuals are compelling. Xavier, head of the X-Men, is depicted as Martin Luther King on trial as a mutant. "We used that image to depict otherness," says Jennings. Spoken-word poet Gil Scott-Heron appears as superhero Gil Scott-Free, a retake on the comic hero and escape artist Scott Free aka Mister Miracle. "It's about breaking free of how people view us," says Jennings. The classic Thor is redesigned as the Mighty Shango, in honor of the Yoruba god. In one illustration, a black power fist emerges in conjunction with the lines "We're not just conscious, we're double conscious," a tongue-in-cheek reference to W. E. B. Du Bois, who coined the philosophy of double consciousness, which argues that African Americans are forever juggling their African and American identities.

But the show also merged black and Jewish experiences. "Jack Kirby and a lot of the comic creators were Jewish. We're looking at the shared experiences between Jewish creators and black creators," says Jennings, noting that both groups wrestle with identity, cultural responsibility, and bias. He adds, "We're looking at the comic space as a space of resistance."

Space is a frequent theme in Afrofuturist art. Whether it's outer space, the cosmos, virtual space, creative space, or physical space, there's this often-understated agreement that to think freely and creatively, particularly as a black person, one has to not just create a work of art, but literally or figuratively create the space to think it up in the first place. The world, it seems, is jam-packed with bought-and-sold rotated images, some as stereotypes and others as counterimages that become stereotypes mounting into watershed debates about "positive" and "negative" images in the media.

The Black Age in Comix

John Jennings is an advocate of using comics to shape black identity and Afrofuturism. In fact, he and Damian Duffy edited the anthology *Black Comix*, an art book featuring the works of dozens of black independent comic artists. "We wanted to look at these types of books done by African American creators and the diversity of things that were offered," Jennings says. But he, like many artists, is charged to add more black images to the visual lexicon. "If you're not white and you're in this country, you're starving for images of yourself."

At the Chicago Comic Con in April 2012, the Institute for Comics Studies hosted a panel on black comic book creators, which I moderated. Panelists included Stanford Carpenter, the cofounder of the Institute for Comics Studies and creator of *Brother-Story*; Mshindo Kuumba, illustrator for *Jaycen Wise* and *The Batman Chronicles*; Ashley Woods, creator of *Millennia Wars*; and Black Age of Comics founder Turtel Onli. Dressed in my Rayla Illmatic costume, I navigated questions for the hundred or so comic fans in the audience. While the questions focused largely on where we are now, I was struck by how happy everyone was to have a space to share their comic bonds and detailed knowledge. They weren't isolated artists carving out a space to exist in an environment that's hostile to black images. For the first time, the attendees seemed to relish the fact that they were a blossoming community with new possibilities.

But the renaissance of black comics is credited largely to artist Turtel Onli. Onli, a Chicago native, began his career as a commercial illustrator and fine artist in the late 1960s. "I was always looking to the future, because I was never content with the things around me," said Onli. "From the time I started my professional career, I coined a term called rhythmism, which incorporates Afrofuturism. I talked about one part sci-fi, one part mysticism, and one part an advanced environment, derived from an Africanized thought pattern. It was about projecting what things could be, through incantation, mysticism, or magic. It was about aesthetically working to have a visual vocabulary for things to come, instead of things that were established."

While working in Paris, Onli was introduced to comics as a sophisticated art form and released a series of comics, even lending his talents to a Parliament/Funkadelic album cover. Onli eventually coined the phrase "Black Age of Comics" and in 1998 launched a convention of the same name to support independent black comic artists. Today, Black Age of Comics is held annually in Chicago, but there's also a Motor City Black Age of Comics and an East Coast Black Age of Comics, with other affiliates across the country.

However, Onli says that today's visuals in Afrofuturism are rooted in the art of the Black Arts movement of the 1960s and '70s. The Black Arts movement was the artistic wing of the black power movement and provided the iconic images in posters, flyers, album covers, and fine arts that defined black. The movement, coupled with the civil rights movement at large, sparked a black consciousness in America, Africa, and the Caribbean, according to Onli. "We wanted to create a black cultural movement that embraced Africa," he says. "A big part of the Black Arts movement was moving from being Negro to black. It was a revolution. The times didn't change, but we the people changed. We refused to be contained."

The evolution to black marked a new era in consciousness in art. It was the first time that black American culture at large named itself and sought to visually celebrate African aesthetics in the pop art styles changing the art scene.

Onli says, "Prior to the black power revolution, anything African was viewed as inferior and was not to be talked about. The black power movement in America changed their thoughts. It was quite liberating, and you can't have creativity without a liberated mind-set." He continues, "I see Afrofuturism as a by-product of how successful the Black Arts movement was," noting that many efforts were made to suppress that movement.

Although artists aren't always excited about labeling their work, Onli feels that naming movements and styles is incredibly important. "If you don't create jazz as a musical form, then it's hard to reach your heights as a jazz genius. But when it comes to visual arts, we're hesitant to speak genre. We speak passion. But there's a difference between Elizabeth Catlett and Vincent van Gogh, and the difference isn't just passion. Catlett is doing many things in her work, it just hasn't been given a name."

Starships, Outkasts, and Dreamin'

When Northwestern University professor Alexander Weheliye thinks back on the early days of the Afrofuturism Listserv and their assemblage of ideas, he says he's most surprised by the explosion of Afrofuturism in the visual arts. "I thought it would be more popular in music videos," he says. However, images that shift from the underground to the mainstream don't always retain their symbolism. A black fist on a T-shirt today, for example, does not necessarily retain the vigor and meaning it held when raised by marchers in the '60s.

"Visual culture can easily be co-opted, without any connection to the source," says D. Denenge Akpem. She stresses, "With black people in particular, we have a long history of amazing stuff that we do being co-opted in piece or whole and making a lot of money for others."

Music videos are the main visuals for today's music. Eclipsing the power of the album and CD covers of old, the music video is the standard marketing vehicle to tell the musical story. When it comes to the synergy between the imagination, technology, and liberation, the video is the ideal musical storytelling format. Music artists incorporate Afrofuturism, cyberculture, and robot aesthetics as well as a healthy dose of Hollywood sci-fi movies into their music videos. While marketing and sales are factors, artists have pulled on the Afrofuturistic aesthetic to underscore aspiration, with some using it as a primary theme in their branding or approach to music.

Lupe Fiasco, who is accompanied by a dancing robot in the video for "Daydreamin'," credits his dad's love of Chicago architecture for his robot adoration. "If you put all the buildings in the city together, they will make a robot!" his father once told him. The image sparked a boyhood fantasy. "I was given a new lens to view my surroundings with, a valuable tool to help me literally transform the normal into the extraordinary," says Fiasco, who's known for his conscious lyrics and verbal dexterity. "It was an exotic and exciting new perspective that has helped build a career and constantly inspires. To this day, I still ponder how it all fits together and which buildings would be arms and which the legs."[4]

Erykah Badu, queen of neo-soul, plays ethereal earth mother, revolutionary, and space cadet. She emerged during Afrofuturism's formation and frequently drops imagery and references to quantum physics, motherships, and revolution in her music and videos. In her music video for the song "Next Lifetime," she follows soul mates from precolonial Africa, to small-town America with the Black Panthers, to a post-year-3000 Africa. Futuristic Africa is utopia, a re-creation of ancient Africa with nature-based practices and universalism all accented with glow-in-the-dark ceremonial paint and traditional head wraps. In the kaleidoscope-infused video for "Jump Up in the Air (Stay There)," images of a meditating Badu floating in time warps through space are juxtaposed with rapper Lil Wayne in smoke clouds. Badu duplicates the glowing finger tap made famous by *E.T.* with Young Money's Wayne, a bond between two artists often viewed as residing on opposite ends of the hip-hop spectrum.

Andre 3000, one half of Outkast, channels Parliament with his colorful costumes. In the song "Prototype," Andre is a white-haired "extra, extra"–terrestrial who lands on Earth with his multiethnic family and falls in love with an earthling and becomes human.

Janelle Monáe's song "Many Moons" depicts android action on her fictional Metropolis. A call to end fascism, Monáe plays each android, and the scene is part fashion show, part slave auction, and part frenetic concert. R&B singer Bilal's song "Robots" is a warning to society to wake up. The video, directed by Mikael Colombu cuts 3-D images of the moon and a manufactured Bilal critiquing a cookie-cutter society.

Pop sentiments have room for Afrofuturism too. Lil Wayne, who has called himself an alien in his songs, recreated scenes from the dream thriller *Inception* and kicks off with a wake-up slap. Nicki Minaj's techno hip-hop song "Starships" has a spacecraft zip over her futuristic, Polynesian-inspired dance party. And the Black Eyed Peas' "Imma Be Rocking That Body" shows the foursome as a digitized version of themselves through a dream sequence of computer-generated music, dancing giant robots, and break dancers.

Sock It to Me: The Rise of Missy Elliott

Entrepreneur Missy Elliott is known for her creative videos, particularly from 2002 to 2008. Both a producer and artist, she defied the glam standards expected of women singers and joined the lineage of women artists who redefined pop-star beauty and didn't rely on trumped-up sex appeal. Elliott didn't sing about space or sci-fi, nor was her music about liberation per se, but she adopted an abstract rap style that used cognitive dissonance in her music videos.

Elliott made her solo music-video debut with a syncopated gamer track version of Ann Peebles's "I Can't Stand the Rain." Hype Williams directed the star-studded project and decked out Elliott in an abstract, black, trash bag–inspired combo. Her rise set the stage for a new era in music videos. Most of her classic videos were directed by Dave Meyers and contain a mix of horror, classic film imagery, sci-fi, historical fantasy, and 1980s hip-hop in surrealist backdrops with the hottest choreographed routines of the day. She mimicked *The Wiz* with dancing hip-hop scarecrows shaking in the glow of a UFO's light in "Pass That Dutch." And she was a rapping astronaut in a Method Man–inspired video game space world with rapper Da Brat in "Sock It 2 Me." In "Lose Control," Elliott established a time-bending alternative history with steampunk-era dancers in overalls and floor-length white skirts grooving to her twenty-first-century hit. The video intercut the sepia-tinged footage with twenty-first-century hip-hop dancers. But Elliott says she was just aiming for the creative heights established by her hero, the King of Pop.

Moonwalker's Rise

No artist has captured the world's imagination like Michael Jackson. Jackson, now regarded as the greatest entertainer of modern times and the quintessential superstar, set a new standard for pop music, broke black music into the global pop sphere, and did so in part with a new media device that revolutionized the industry: the music video. The video for "Thriller," a highly choreographed mini horror flick with popping-and-locking, groove-loving zombies elevated what was once a simple music promo tool into a bona fide art form. Although Jackson is not regarded as Afrofuturistic in the vein of Sun Ra or Parliament, largely because he didn't sing about space or use his lyrics to invert reality, he did sing music of inspiration, universal love, humanity, earth consciousness, and innocence. His videos are science-and-magic hybrids with fantastic optical illusions.

His mix of dance, music, and showmanship revolutionized the music video, and he frequently integrated fantasy, horror, science fiction, and space themes in his eye-popping all-ages work. Simply put, his videos and television appearances were global events.

And he used dreams to inform his songwriting. "I wake up from dreams and go, 'Wow, put this down on paper,'" he once told *Rolling Stone*. "The whole thing is strange. You hear the words, everything is right there in front of your face."[5]

Motown 25, an anniversary celebration honoring the biggest names in music, is remembered most for Jackson's debut of the Moonwalk, a backward-gliding dance that has minds boggled to this day. The dance became his staple, and millions of people around the world tried, with varying degrees of success, to replicate it. A decade before, he recorded "Dancing Machine" with the Jackson 5 and debuted a kinetic version of the dance the Robot on *Soul Train*. No one can dance like Michael Jackson, and no one championed appropriately named space-era sci-fi dances like him either.

Jackson was always larger than life, and throughout his career he revved up fantastical futuristic possibilities. "I believe in wishes and in a person's ability to make a wish come true. I really do. And a wish is more than a wish, it's a goal that your conscious and subconscious can help make a reality," he said.

Michael Jackson's *Moonwalker*, a ninety-minute musical movie, is a wonderland fantasy that follows Jackson dancing as a "smooth criminal" figure and later exploding Transformers-style into a gigantic spaceship. "Scream," his popular duet with sister Janet, was inspired by *2001: A Space Odyssey*. The twosome danced and played video games in a minimalistic space station that resembled a mini CD player. The grandiosity and timelessness of his music and videos make him feel immortal. In Sega's video game *Space Channel 5*, he appears as Space Michael, a character whose dance moves "transcend time and space." How fitting that on his posthumous *Michael* album the symbolic collage includes a hovering spacecraft.

9

A CLOCK FOR
TIME
TRAVELERS

There's something about African American culture in particular that dictates that all cultural hallmarks and personal evolutions are recast in a historical lineage. Whether it's the concept of prophesy and speaking into the future or tropes of the past shadowing the present, whether by need or by narrative, many speak as if the future, past, and present are one. The threads that bind can be as divergent as a tersely worded tweet, musical chord, fiery speech, ancient Kemetic symbol, Bible quote, starry night, or string theory, but there's an idea that the power of thought, word, and the imagination can somehow transcend time. Just as the right words and actions can speak the future into existence, the same can recast the past, too. This cyclical nature of time and the contemplation of it all is a favorite theme and conversation point for Afrofuturists.

Time travel is a popular theme in science fiction. From H. G. Wells's *The Time Machine* to the classic film *Back to the Future*, the ideas of rewinding the clock or fast-forwarding into the future have piqued the curiosity of the world's best minds, creators, and scientists. In fact, the ideas are so ingrained in pop culture that the common time-zapping themes are nearly cliche. How many characters have leapfrogged into the past to "fix" some wrong only to screw up the future and be forced to DeLorean their way back again? How many times has a well-meaning attempt to alter time trapped the main character in a series of parallel universes? The morals and ethics have been tossed about by sci-fi fans and pop culture lovers alike. Even the new-school fields of quantum physics and quantum mechanics are based on the likely premise that time is relative. The popularity of documentaries like *What the Bleep Do We Know!?*, about quantum physics and new discoveries about space and time, provides more proof of the abundant probabilities of jetting through the here and now.

"What physicists are discovering right now is so bizarre it almost sounds like science fiction, like we're not talking about science anymore," said Fred Alan Wolf—aka Dr. Quantum—physicist and author.[1]

Time travel, parallel universes, the multiverse, and the Higgs boson are on a fast-track collision with the best in sci-fi. Time travel dominates Afrofuturism as well. Whether it's a lighthearted comic book about a time-traveling family or Sun Ra using time travel as a musical device as revealed in the film *Space Is the Place*, time travel is a broadly accepted tool in most Afrofuturistic works.

But for Afrofuturists, the notion of bending time erases the prism of race-based limitations that all too often lace the present and define the recent past. "I think we feel held hostage to time," says D. Denenge Akpem, professor and artist. "There's this idea that if you can control time and your place in it, you can control the course of history and your own history. Afrofuturists create new visions. If you can create a new vision of the future, you can create a new vision of the past." Time travel also alleviates regret, she adds: "It's about empowerment; you're reshaping yourself, reshaping reality."

Parallel dimensions that can be channeled through music, desire, and thought are common themes among Afrofuturist artists. "A lot of people feel trapped in time and look at it as linear," says Rasheedah Phillips, founder of the AfroFuturist Affair, a nonprofit arts collective in Philadelphia. "They feel like they have no control over the future or the past. The main thing with me doing Afrofuturism is helping to look at time as a cycle and use that and the past for change. How can I use those cycles in a way that is more powerful for me to change my future?"

Time-Warped Wonders

Jaycen Wise is one of the most popular African American characters in independent comics. He defies limitations of time and space with his gift of immortality. Wise, a scholar and warrior, is the "hero's hero" and the "last son of the African Empire of Kush." He must battle ignorance while preserving light and knowledge. He can be in a battle in ancient Egypt or rescuing prized diamonds in modern-day Manhattan; Wise has the ability to be anywhere. "I have a passion for developing cutting edge material that pushes the boundaries of the imagination," says Uraeus, the creator of Jaycen Wise, in the book *Black Comix*.[2]

One of the great dilemmas in the development of black characters in sci-fi is the question of handling race in the modern context. Time travel, immortality, reincarnation, and parallel universes create wormholes to supersede limitations of history while restoring power to both the narrative and its readers. The gaping hole of history and knowledge that Afrofuturism fills with fantasy and the multiverse embraces the greatest power a story can hold by reinstituting the ultimate hero's journey.

When Dr. Quantum was asked about the lessons of possible time travel and his scientific discoveries, he said, "The past is being created as much as the future. Once you get yourself into the position of creating the past, present, and future, rather than just being a victim of the past you become a magician."[3] Sun Ra would feel vindicated. He's not alone.

"Time is not linear," says graphic novelist Radi Lewis. "I think it folds in on itself. You can close your eyes and go back to a memory of when you're a kid; who's to say you're not going back in time?" Lewis wrote the graphic novel *Children of the Phoenix*. "I based it around my family, wife, and dog," says the New York native, who recently relocated to Arizona. Children of the Phoenix follows the Phoenix family, a reincarnated version of Adam and Eve who are deemed the protectors of their five children. "It sounds corny, but I kind of feel that way about my wife. I've known my wife since I was fourteen years old," says Lewis. They aren't immortal, says Lewis of his characters, but much like energy, "you can't destroy them, and they'll just reappear in another form. A secret race tracks the family down each incarnation and they sacrifice themselves for humanity."

A Time to Heal

No one wants to revisit the atrocities of slavery in the antebellum South. Forget the scariness of a dystopian future; the transatlantic slave trade is a reminder of where collective memories don't want to go, even if the trip is in their imagination. But Octavia Butler defied time-travel norms by sending her heroine into American slavery in her epic work *Kindred*. "The immediate effect of reading Octavia Butler's *Kindred* is to make every other time travel book in the world look as if it's wimping out," writes Jo Walton on Tor.com.[4]

Butler's character Dana leaves her comfy life in 1976 California and is transported to a slave plantation in 1815. She faces her ancestors, including a young boy with a slave mother and slave-master father. Survival is her greatest triumph.

Slavery is neither the utopian future nor an ancient far-removed past. The tragedy that split the nation into warring factions has effects that can be felt in the politics of the present. Slavery is feared. The historic hot potato, there is no romanticized imagery that makes for fictitious time-travel stories in the antebellum South that aren't emotional firestorms. Slavery is a stone's throw away from exploring death, and even death writhes with freedom.

One of the greatest achievements of Quentin Tarantino's 2012 film *Django Unchained*—a slave revenge story told as part spaghetti western, part romance, and part action film—was the fact that a Hollywood hero story where the black former slave wins could even be told in the antebellum South and be historically relevant, entertaining, and relatable. The film defied all conventions and was a critically acclaimed blockbuster. Butler's book *Kindred* was published in 1979—but only after being rejected by many publishers, most of whom didn't understand how a sci-fi novel could take place in such an uncomfortable time and have a black hero. Butler made her point, a declaration of humanity and social justice, and the result is a classic.

The book likely has inspired other slave-based time-travel tales. For example, the independent movie *Sankofa*, directed by Haile Gerima, follows Mona, a model who has a photo shoot at a Ghanian slave castle that held captured Africans before shipping them to the Americas. Mona is instantly transported through time, survives the Middle Passage, and becomes a slave who eventually aligns with a rebellious West Indian plotting to rebel. Both Dana and Mona, who had been relatively disengaged from social issues and history, return to their modern worlds with a greater understanding of their slave and African lineage.

Butler argued that *Kindred* wasn't technically sci-fi because Dana didn't use scientific means to travel. The same can be said of Mona in *Sankofa*, yet both Butler and Gerima used time travel as a tool to ingrain the realities of slave life and the ensuing sense of responsibility into their protagonists. They used time travel to encourage connections to a painful past.

"Reasons" circa Earth, Wind & Fire

Time travel is a fun way to free black characters from the restrictions of the times. But the time-travel element transcends storytelling and is a popular, albeit unidentified, practice taken up by musicians and theorists alike.

"As African Americans and blacks in the diaspora, we think cyclically," says musician Shawn Wallace. "We view time cyclically. We usually return to something in the past to interpret it. That's almost how we create our music; we go back to something and see how we can do it differently. Let's speed it up, let's slow it down." Wallace points to Maurice White of Earth, Wind & Fire and the band's use of the kalimba, sometimes called the African thumb piano. "He took a very simple instrument that opened him up rhythmically and it changed his music. We're always going back to go forward."

Almost reminiscent of Torah Midrash methods, a method of analyzing Hebrew text, Afrofuturists are constantly recontextualizing the past in a way that changes the present and the future. Sometimes seemingly distant occurrences are linked as an evolution of liberation consciousness. President Obama's election is recast as a manifestation of Dr. Martin Luther King's legacy. Hope is a deep-rooted catchphrase anchored by President Obama that was echoed with as much fervor by Rev. Jesse Jackson and Dr. King before him. If you read passages by Malcolm X, Marcus Garvey, and Frederick Douglass, you'd think you're reading the same person. How are these voices linked, and how do they inform the future? Is the narrative stronger that the speakers themselves?

"We're constantly trying to figure out how we got here," says Wallace. "We are still grappling with how quickly our lives have changed as Americans and African Americans—how within my lifetime our family structure has so drastically shifted. I'm not saying one is better than another, I'm just noting a difference. Well, how did we get here, what music was the soundtrack? What theater were we into? What dances were we doing? What was our cultural output when we got to a certain point in our lives? Can we go back to that? I think, too, because of our particular experience in America, we're still piecing ourselves together and we're constantly going back to grab a piece as we move forward."

Photographer Alisha Wormsley is working on her Reverse Migration Project. She writes, "In the interest of time travel, I'm following the reverse order of my ancestral migration. It will go something like this: Pittsburgh—Appalachian Mountains—Virginia—North Carolina—South Carolina—Barbados—Cape (Slave) Coast, West Africa. Then I will make something."

Ancient to the Future

The continent of Africa frequently serves as the alpha and omega of motherlands, a cosmic metaphor for a utopian future and the past. It's evident in Afrofuturistic comic art, music, and literature.

The AACM's motto is "Ancient to the Future," and they work to play and teach the ancient musical healing traditions combined with the instruments of the past and today. "[Music] is a portal for time travel in a literal and figurative way," says Khari B., president of the AACM.

"For an African American who's never left America, Africa feels like the future," says musician Morgan Craft, who believes that great things will emerge from the continent. It's the reason you'll see graphic images of characters like Mshindo Kuumba's stunning illustration of Aniku, a mask-wearing, sword-wielding man with samurai leanings, or Demeke, a man in a golden cloak and African staff, and it's not clear whether they're images from the ancient African past or figures on a far-off planet in the future. "I think we as black artists are trying to come to grips with our epic past and what it could be again. The Garden of Eden of the future is in Africa," says Craft.

"It's that sankofa effect," says Khari B., referring to the Asante image of a bird that looks backward with the egg of the future on her back. He adds, "One step into the future while looking back. It's not that we're going backward, but we're evolving using the strength and characteristics of things that are why we're here today. We get to pull from our past to build our future. That's what Afrofuturism is about, going back to ancient traditions so that we can move more correctly into the future."

But the idea of time travel, oddly enough, also reemphasizes the present. "Not being able to literally fold time, how do we think about time travel in the present?" asks Stacey Robinson, artist and cocreator of the *Black Kirby* exhibit. "What do we do in the present?" he asks, adding that staying in the present tense reemphasizes responsibility. Even the hypothetical time-travel concept still alters the present. He says, "I would approach time travel as an extension of the person traveling. How would time travel affect me?"

Robinson is correct. If today is future's past, what does that say about the present? Who are we in real time?

10

THE SURREAL
LIFE

Poet and artist D. Scot Miller was intrigued by Afrofuturism. As an advisor to the experimental journal *Nocturnes Literary Review*, Miller was immersed in the genre at the onset. The San Francisco resident frequented Alondra Nelson's Afrofuturism Listserv and later consulted with the East Coast collective the Black Futurists. But when Miller began writing his book *Knot Frum Hear*, he wasn't sure if Afrofuturism was the best way to describe the endeavor. "It's like science fiction, but it's not. It's like fantasy, but it happens in real time," he said, recalling attempts to describe it to friends. It wasn't until he read Black Arts movement vanguard Amiri Baraka's introduction to Henry Dumas's *Ark of Bones and Other Stories* that he discovered the term Afro-surreal.

Baraka claimed that Dumas's hybrid mystical lens is Afro-surreal. Dumas "created an entirely different world organically connected to this one," Baraka writes. "They are morality tales, magical resonating dream emotions and images, shifting ambiguous terror, mystery, implied revelation," writes Baraka in his essay "Henry Dumas: Afro-Surreal Expressionist." He continues, "But they are also stories of real life, now or whenever, constructed in weirdness and poetry in which the contemporaneousness of essential themes is clear." Afro-surreal would come to explain the southern folklore and magic of Zora Neale Hurston as well as the hauntings and history of Toni Morrison.

Afro-surreal triggered a new worldview for Miller too. It described the mystical, present-day leanings in his work. In 2002 Miller reached out to Baraka and interviewed him. Impressed with Miller's excitement, Baraka encouraged the young poet. "He said I was open to continue to explore and continue to open up doors," Miller says. "It was like wind at my back. I took it pretty seriously."

Miller, a pop culture writer, wrote a bevy of essays on art and referenced Afro-surrealism as he saw it appear in film and music. "My editor said, 'OK, what is it?' and that's how we came up with the Afro-surrealism edition of the *San Francisco Bay Guardian*." The edition ran in 2009 and featured essays and art from the likes of Greg Tate, known for his hip-hop and Afrofuturism critiques, and Amy Wiley. But it was Miller's "Afrosurrealism Manifesto" that became the anchor for a new wave of surrealists. Referencing the Harlem Renaissance in the 1920s and the Negritude movement by black francophones, Miller argued that Afro-surrealism, in all its fantastic forms, is not Afrofuturism, nor is it surrealism. The first world and third world have collapsed, says the manifesto. What we live in today is the Afro-surreal.

"Afro-surrealists expose this from a 'future-past' called right now," writes Miller. "Right now, Barack Hussein Obama is America's first black president. Right now, Afro-surreal is the best description to the reactions, the genuflections, the twists and the unexpected turns this 'browning' of White-Straight-Male-Western-Civilization has produced."

"I honestly believe it's the in-betweens," Miller says. "It's outside of everyone's comfort zone."

The manifesto's tenets celebrate the invisible world and nature, the absurd and the whimsical, in depicting the beauties and dichotomies of the day. "Afro-surrealists use excess as the only legitimate means of subversion and hybridization as a form of disobedience," Miller writes. "Afro-surrealists strive for rococo: the beautiful, the sensuous, and the whimsical." With a penchant for masks, dandyism, and eighteenth-century aesthetics, Afro-surrealism decontextualizes the day. To quote surrealist poets Aime and Suzanne Cesaire, Afro-surrealism sparkles with "the marvelous." The emphasis on today rather than the future, the minimal tech, heavy folklore, and mystical prism, according to Miller, makes an aesthetic all its own.

Miller is on to something. These are surreal times. President Obama's election and the countermovements, extremist media, and confusion of analysts and journalists who just can't reconcile what they were seeing without dropping dated lingo of the past would read as the sci-fi of yesteryear. Today the reelection of a black president, gay marriage, legalized marijuana, the war against women's fertility rights, violent outbreaks, the Arab Spring, class didactics, and the browning of America are causing some serious reevaluation, and the outbreak of fuming anger juxtaposed with excitable glee makes for great art.

Saturday Night Live made history with their record-breaking political parodies, but most of the laughable skits were verbatim quotes from presidential debates and press conferences. No satire needed. If you followed the chair debacle from the 2012 Republican National Convention, at which actor Clint Eastwood berated an empty chair, supposedly talking to the president in an attempt at improv theater, you've seen the surreal. Thousands of people took to their cell phones and iPads, tweeting photos of themselves waving a finger at an empty La-Z-Boy during the convention, to which President Obama's feed responded with a photo of him seated in a White House chair, back to the audience, full ears in profile, and the caption, "This seat's taken." It's the ultimate slam-dunk tweet. The next day, all the political media talked about was Eastwood's chair episode. Forget the party platform, forget the other speakers that night; the chair stole the show. It could all read like a bizarro-world alternative history if it weren't reality. Capturing the dramatic victories and the about-face politics in all their folkloric glory in real time is Afro-surrealism.

In fact, Miller says he couldn't have written his manifesto without President Obama's polar shift. "It highlights so much of the module change that has taken place, and the absurdities of the outcomes of that change. Like when Bill O'Reilly said America is no longer a white nation . . . America hasn't been a white nation in a long time."

Now and Forever

When I think about Afro-surrealism, I think of divvying up Sun Ra's work into a right brain/left brain, masculine/feminine hybrid, with, say, his love of all things futuristic, space-bound, and electric on one side and his African mythmaking, metaphysics, and real-world efforts to heal through music on the other.

The attempt to divide him in two is very sci-fi, but it makes for a great example. Afro-surrealism, as Miller frames it, is low-tech, present-day, and sees very little difference between the dream world and the waking one. "For other cultures dream time and real time is the same time. This idea that dreams are premonitions, all of us do that," Miller says.

"It's not about tapping into the subconscious, but you're already tapped in to that. You're bringing in the dream, the fantasy and the marvelous. While you're asleep and awake you are manifesting. People have to be able to transform their living situation."

The genre differs from surrealism only in the highly mystical bent. Leopold Senghor, Senegal's first president and also a poet, saw a difference between early black surrealists and their European contemporaries, believing that European surrealism was "empirical" while African surrealism was "mystical and metaphorical."

What else is Afro-surreal? Kehinde Wiley's Renaissance-style paintings of modern-day black men with the flower-tinged backgrounds and Kara Walker's infamous Victorian-style silhouettes of slave-era stereotypes fall within this vein, says Miller. Wale takes men with hip-hop swag and poses them like the French kings, knights, and dukes of the sixteenth and seventeenth centuries. Walker's silhouettes, despite their popularity, are harshly criticized as profane and offensive for their large-scale size and the freakish sex and violence.

"With Afro-surreal, it allows us to address the absurdity head-on," says Miller. "That's why. Kara Walker has an understanding of the absurdity of it. Sometimes you have to be irreverent. Sometimes the situation is so absurd that the only way to address it is to be absurd."

Artist Nick Cave's *Soundsuits* exhibit, a hybrid of monster-size wearable art and sculpture is Afro-surreal. Writer Johnny Ray Huston described them as "acid-trip Bigfoot creatures." A former Alvin Ailey dancer and chair of the School of the Art Institute of Chicago's fashion department, Cave made the giant ensembles from natural and artificial materials.

Rapper Nicki Minaj's cartoonish high fashion, neon wigs, comical expressions, and multiple personalities; the social commentary, spaghetti western violence, and humor in Quentin

Tarantino's *Django Unchained*; the mythology in the post-Katrina narrative *Beasts of the Southern Wild*; even the over-the-top irreverent antics in rapper Trinidad James's near-ridiculous video for "All Gold Everything" are evidence of the Afro-surreal in pop culture.

Afro-surrealism also flirts with sexual ambiguity, one of the tenets in Miller's manifesto. The androgyny and dandyism of pop star Prince (who pioneered the seventeenth-century French aesthetic in 1980s fashion) is a strong influence. But Afro-surrealism relishes ambiguity in general. In Ralph Ellison's *Invisible Man*, Rinehart the runner, a dandy pimp, snakes through a fluid underworld as a prophetic underlord who brings light to a world that the main character has never seen, thus blurring reality. Miller says that Rinehart's trademark sunglasses and hat are masks. Masks are treasured in the Afro-surreal—the more gothic and indigenous, the better. Why? The mask is magical, draws wearers out of their conventions. But Afro-surrealism isn't always over the top. The theater of Suzan-Lori Parks and her contemporary plays about black life are also under the Afro-surreal banner.

"Afro-Surrealism rejects the quiet servitude that characterizes existing roles for African Americans, Asian Americans, Latinos, women and queer folk. Only through the mixing, melding and cross-conversion of these supposed classifications can there be hope for liberation. Afro-Surrealism is intersexed, Afro-Asiatic, Afro-Cuban, mystical, silly and profound," write Miller.

Today, many artists who create Afro-surreal writing and art are also Afrofuturists. Just as Sun Ra embodies both aesthetics (he wouldn't have called himself Afrofuturist or Afro-surreal), so do the new wave of artists working in the twenty-first century.

But like Sun Ra, even those who describe themselves as both often have a hard time separating the two ideals in their work. "I actually like that struggle, that both of these terms are very much still being defined," says Krista Franklin, a renowned collagist interviewed by Sixty Inches From the Center. "I'm a science fiction geek and I love horror and the supernatural, so it makes a lot of sense for my work to be described as Afrofuturist and Afro-surrealist."

The two are flipsides of the same coin, with shared influences and champions. Today, the two aesthetics are so intertwined that it's nearly impossible to talk about one without talking about the other. For the Afrofuturist, the future can be mystical and technology can be mythical. As a society, we're hardwired to technology we can't live without, from Google Maps and satellites to energy pipelines that heat our homes. We are technology dependent today. In this space-time continuum where the future is now, the idea of the present gets sticky. But the best distinction is that Afrofuturism is more tech-heavy and races between the future and the distant past, whereas Afro-surrealism is low-tech and placed squarely in today, though it has a serious infatuation with seventeenth-century fashion and masks.

Ark of the Bones

Henry Dumas is one of the vanguards for new age Afro-surrealists. An unsung poet with a growing cult following, he was born July 20, 1934, in Sweet Water, Alabama. He quickly became one of the emerging writers in Harlem's Black Arts scene. Sun Ra and prolific writer Amiri Baraka were friends of his. But Dumas's work was uniquely different from the work surfacing in the Black Arts movement of the time. A former airman in the air force, Dumas was introduced to Sufism and Arab arts and myths while stationed in Saudi Arabia. Combining his longtime fascination with folklore and his studies of mysticism, Dumas wove both into poems and stories about contemporary love and life. Through Dumas's lens, the fantastic and magical were treasures of daily life, and he wrote the ordinary and extraordinary as a through line for the contemporary black experience. His work appeared in black literary magazines, including the *Negro Digest* and the *Liberator*. And he was one of the contributors to the black liberation anthology edited by Baraka and culturist Larry Neal. "Ark of Bones" is Dumas's most popular story. When an ark lands in an Arkansas river, Headeye is initiated to claim his destiny as the head of the ship. The ship itself contains the bones of black people who died in the Middle Passage or through other racist means.

Those who chronicle Dumas's life note that he and Sun Ra were very close, swapping mystical insights, cultural nuggets, and their own theories on art's role in shaping the culture of the day. Dumas was heavily influenced by Sun Ra's takes on space, and Sun Ra was captivated by southern folklore. They shared an inquiry into the esoteric. In the spring of 1968, after leaving one of Sun Ra's band's sessions, Dumas, then a married father of two, was murdered by a policeman in a New York subway. It was a case of mistaken identity. Dumas was thirty-three.

Friend and poet Eugene Redmond painstakingly championed Dumas's work and memory. In 1974 he edited *Ark of Bones and Other Stories* and later assembled other anthologies of Dumas's poems, stories, and unfinished novels. Today Dumas has a cult following, and Toni Morrison claims that he's a literary genius.

In 2009 historian Robin Kelley and surrealist Franklin Rosemont compiled *Black, Brown, & Beige: Surrealist Writings from Africa and the Diaspora*, the most comprehensive book on black surreal movements around the world. The book traces the Negritude movement back to the Martinican students in France, led by Etienne Lero, and *Legitimate Defense*, a journal published in 1932; it also includes the surrealist influences on Richard Wright. Ralph Ellison's *Invisible Man* is deemed Afro-surrealist. Beat poet Bob Kaufman and poet/ artist Ted Joans emerged in the black power movement as well. Both were self-described surrealists, and Kaufman is now credited as a forerunner in the spoken word movement.

Together *Black, Brown, & Beige* and "The Afrosurrealism Manifesto" are the pillars of emerging Afro-surreal works today. The Dumas/Sun Ra connection and their shared use of myth, mysticism, and culture forever connect the aesthetics.

Inspired by Miller's manifesto, Alexandria Eregbu curated *Marvelous Freedom / Vigilance of Desire, Revisited* at Columbia College in Chicago. The show, which ran from January to March, 2013, highlighted emerging black artists who create the Afro-surreal. But it also was an ode to the epic Chicago Surrealist Group and the 1976 exhibition *Marvelous Freedom / Vigilance of Desire*, the largest show of its kind. The 2013 show included works by Krista Franklin, Devin Cain, Stephen Flemister, Christina Long, Cecil McDonald Jr., Kenrick McFarlane, Hannah Rodriguez, Chelsea Sheppard, Michael Tousana, Cameron Welch, and avery r. young.

The Afro-surreal canon is growing. There's an Afro-surrealist film festival in Negril, Jamaica, that was started in 2010, a DC samba band recently adopted the name Afro-Surreal, and Franklin presented the manifesto at Columbia College in Chicago. Other writers are taking Miller's lead, adopting the Afro-surreal lens too.

"I'm really excited about the Afro-surreal work that's out here," says Miller. His job won't be done until the manifesto manifests, he says. Afro-surrealism draws a line in the sand when it comes to the virtues of the present versus the future, which echoes Sun Ra's popular belief that the much-ballyhooed end of the world already happened. Whether the future is now or the past is the future really depends on the actions taken today.

AGENT
CHANGE

At heart, artists always hope to move their viewers. They hope their work gives some meaningful thought to ponder or at least shines a floodlight on matters ignored. And there are those who expect their radical fiction and flicks to be calls to action, spurring readers and viewers to change course, jump ship, or move with the techno beat of new times.

Controversial author Sam Greenlee likes to say that his only regret regarding his book *The Spook Who Sat by the Door,* a story about a black government agent who leads a revolution, is that he didn't do it himself. But artists like Greenlee aren't the norm. Most artists, fiction writers, etc., while having some intention for the viewer, are in a constant state of flux with the meteoric transference of ideas and how they blossom once they hit the main stage. I'm sure the *Star Trek* creators weren't thinking that by casting a black woman in their sci-fi series they would inspire the first black woman astronaut, although they knew it would somehow alter the face of race dynamics. I would guess that while Henry Dumas yearned to end inequality, he didn't know his short stories would birth a genre dubbed the Afro-surreal. What would an artist do if they knew audiences were hungry to use their work for real world social change?

"I was mind-blown by anyone who used art as real world planning," said N. K. Jemisin. "It can be helpful or inhibiting to know that someone is trying to use my work for real world application. It could fill me with horror, or I would become more conscious." Jemisin said she views activists as people who put their lives on the line; to know that her work could contribute to that is a larger-than-life responsibility almost too awesome to comprehend.

There are many activists who look to Afrofuturism and the canon of literature and theories as a platform for social change and the stoking of the imagination. Adrienne Maree Brown, Colleen Coleman, and Rasheedah Phillips are three women in three different urban communities, but they share a belief that triggering the imagination through tales about the future compels thinkers to break out of their circumstances.

An Imagination Rekindled

In 2011 I attended the Think Galacticon conference. Unlike the typical science fiction conference, the creators of Think Galacticon hoped to use science fiction as a platform for broader changes in society. Held at Chicago's Roosevelt University, the conference brought activists, science fiction writers, and fans together to share new perspectives on social change and privilege. Panels included talks on classism in fantasy novels (Why don't the paupers ever challenge the prince for power?), the growing black independent comic book scene, and personal growth tools for the revolution.

Both the panels and attendees were incredibly enthusiastic. A cross-cultural assemblage of radical activists and sci-fi fans, they were excited to attend the workshop and chat run by noted activist Adrienne Maree Brown.

"It's amazing to change the world, but it's heartbreaking, bone-cracking work, and you often don't see the change in real time," Brown says. "For me as an organizer, what gets me through has been immersing myself into these sci-fi worlds." She uses sci-fi to frame an inspirational perspective for youth that she works with too. "Your life is science fiction," she's told them. "You are sci-fi, you are Luke Skywalker but way cooler; you're trans and black and you're surviving the world of Detroit."

Brown began her activism work in college. She is a former executive director of the Ruckus Society, a nonprofit that specializes in environmental activism and guerilla communication, and is heavily involved with the League of Pissed Off Voters. A Detroit resident, she describes herself as an organizational healer, pleasure activist, and artist and is "obsessed" with learning and developing models for action and community transformation.

But she's also a sci-fi fan. After discovering Octavia Butler's work, she was inspired to develop new work of her own. Brown is using Butler's pivotal series *The Parables* and its postapocalyptic tale of discovery as a template for change agency in desperate communities. Her workshop at Think Galacticon was titled "Octavia Butler and Emergent Strategies." And the workshop description read as follows:

> "All that you touch, you change. All that you change, changes you. The only lasting truth is change. God is change." These words of Octavia Butler's have impacted people very seriously on a personal level—but how do we apply her wisdom on a political organizing level? How do we approach the strategic planning we're all supposed to do if we accept, and come to love, the emergent power of changing conditions? This session will be half popular organizational development training, half inquiry into what the future of organizational development and strategic planning will look like.

As far as Brown is concerned, many abandoned urban communities are postapocalyptic in nature. Such places are rife for community-born transformation. "If you look at cities in the US right now, there are cities or communities in apocalyptic situations," says Brown. She references challenged areas in New York City, New Orleans in the aftermath of Katrina, Cincinnati, and her new home, Detroit. "Detroit used to be this booming industry town. This used to be a big, booming factory town. You could make a living here, probably a better living if you were a black person than most other places. Now there's seven hundred thousand living in the city proper. That's a huge shift."

When Brown first arrived, her first impression was that Detroit was in a postapocalyptic state. The town felt as if it had been abandoned, she said. But slowly she recognized the supports and humanity. "It made me look at other cities [with blighted communities] differently. There are people living in places that we associate with the end of the world, but it's not the end of the world, it's the beginning of something else. An economy based on relationships and not the monetary value you can place on someone else."

In fact, Brown now teaches activists how to use strategies from Butler's books to build communities in areas where resources are scarce. She presented a workshop on her strategies at the conference. Such strategies include community farming, building relationships with neighbors, and essential survival skills.

She emphasizes that people in troubled areas need to have self-determination over their food supply. She says, "In *The Parables* Butler talks about the Acorn communities—it's an intentional community, a place where people come in an intentional way to build a life together. They are farming and they have some accountability to one another. They have a spiritual community. I feel that is one strategy that's laid out as one of the ways to survive a future where our resources are unsure."

She adds, "Another is door-to-door relationship building that is nonjudgmental. After the Acorn community is trashed, instead of the main character feeling smashed, she goes door-to-door and starts to build a community of believers who are not rooted in one place, but rooted in a shared ideology. It's very similar to the Zapatista ideology. They went around for ten years building relationships one by one. Now a lot of organizing is done around the Internet and tweeting each other. If we weren't able to do that, what would we do? We would work with whoever is there with us."

She's also a big advocate of teaching essential survival skills that are necessary in postapocalyptic circumstances, including gardening, basic care for the sick and wounded, and serving as a midwife. "I'm also looking at building homes and bathrooms. How do you make a bathroom where there is none?" she asks.

While some might challenge the apocalyptic comparison, Brown argues that her main point is to generate solutions. "We shouldn't spend the majority of our time trying to get someone else to be accountable for what happens to our communities," she says. "What I like about Octavia is that there are so many people working outside of the system in her works. She says, 'Don't wait for someone to do it for you; you provide the solutions yourself.' That apocalyptic situation is not something that someone else is going to get you out of; you have to lift yourself out of that."

However, Brown has also found that the creation of science fiction by fellow activists is also a great way to keep activists and advocates motivated. "An activist can work on an issue, and the result won't come until after their lifetime," says Brown. She adds that the work, while rewarding, can sometimes feel never-ending. Exploring the future through science fiction can be a great support and healing tool, she says. In fact, she's currently gathering works of science fiction from activists for a collection.

"What is the biggest story we can imagine telling ourselves and say about our future?" Brown posed to her colleagues. "It can be a utopia, a dystopia, but we wanted to get a perspective from people who are actually trying to change the world today. I'm really curious, what do they think will happen? What do they think is the best-case scenario? How do we get people to think of themselves as creators of tomorrow's story?

Imagine a World

One year, while teaching art to a group of students in a troubled inner-city area, Colleen Coleman wanted to discuss a made-for-TV film that had aired the night before. She felt the film, an apocalyptic tale where only a few suburbanites survived, would stimulate an interesting discussion about survival and fortitude. To her surprise, the students resolved that if such a horror occurred, they would probably perish. She says, "I remember kids coming into the school saying, 'We're just going to die. It's just going to be over.' There was this certain apathy. They felt they had no control."

It's a sentiment she felt intensified after 9/11 and is only complicated by the proliferation of drugs in many communities and returning soldiers and families who are wrestling with PTSD. However, Coleman, a recent graduate of the School of the Art

Institute of Chicago, did her thesis on Afrofuturism. She believes that Afrofuturism can stimulate the imagination and give many kids the confidence to hope and expect more.

"Afrofuturism allows you to play," she says. Coleman was one of several teaching artists who worked with elementary and high school students to create art using Afrofuturism at the Museum of Contemporary African Diasporan Arts (MoCADA) in Brooklyn. Coleman found that many of her students over the years weren't in touch with their imaginations. She says, "There's a lack of creativity being germinated, and it has to do with being taught to the test. Teachers don't have time to introduce young people to their imagination."

Coleman is now one of the teaching artists at the MoCADA, which is known for innovative workshops and exhibits. For the past twelve years, they have hosted a culminating art exhibit for the Artists-in-Schools Program, their twenty-to-thirty-week arts partnership with public schools in the neighborhood. They typically work with seven schools a year. "Most of our students' schools don't have art programs," says Ruby Amanze, MoCADA director of education. The theme of the culminating art show changes from year to year, and the 2012 theme was a new one for the museum and the students: Afrofuturism.

The children were asked to visualize the future and to create collective art projects. One group of students created a large door symbolizing a passageway into the future. Another used photography to depict how they wanted to be remembered in the future. Others recreated what black music would sound like. While the artwork was intriguing, the processes that led to the creation of the work were incredible. "Although it's a visual art program, 80 percent of the focus includes a historical focus," says Amanze. She adds, "At one school the teacher asked the boys how they would feel if the girls told their history and wrote out the boys. The boys were really upset at the thought of it." But the discussion compelled many of the children to give some serious thought to the future, their connection to the future now, and the impact of the past.

"I use Afrofuturism to get students to talk about their future," says Coleman. "[Many] have a difficult time seeing a future. For some reason, the future is a blur, as if they live in the land where time stands still." But she stimulates their minds. "I ask them why companies are building space stations. I ask them about the idea of people being intergalactic tourists and who will be able to afford it," she says. "We talk about running out of water. I think they understand that there are dire issues that we have to address in the world. I'm hoping that by having these conversations, they will begin to think about what they can do for themselves as individuals and collectively how they can build a new society. I think it can open up a lot of possibilities."

Reawakening and Prisons

Rasheedah Phillips launched the AfroFuturist Affair in 2011. A member of the Black Science Fiction Society, she wanted to create a community of artists in Philadelphia who could gather and share their work. The event began as an open-mic featuring writers and poets but soon evolved into a larger community of shared interests. Phillips hosted a charity and costume ball as well as an Afrofuturism lecture featuring women performance artists.

When I spoke with her, she had just completed a workshop with recently released inmates who were in a work-reentry program.

"It was amazing," she says. "Part of my mission is to spread the word about what Afrofuturism is beyond groups of intellectuals. I wanted to introduce this to people who might not have access to this audience." Phillips won a micro-grant for the AfroFuturist Affair and, while presenting at the awards dinner, was asked to share her work at a reentry program. The participants in the reentry program ranged from their mid-twenties to late fifties. Most were men, a few were women. Most were black.

"I opened the workshop by asking them what was their favorite sci-fi-themed book or TV show," says Phillips. "I asked them to tell me in one sentence how they saw their future or what they thought would happen a hundred years from now." Then she talked about racism in science fiction and how they felt about not seeing their image in media. "They were so into it," she says. "They really schooled me, and in terms of breaking down core concepts, they were on top of it."

Next Phillips talked about breaking cycles and looking to the past and present to identify patterns that no longer worked in their life. She used the metaphor of a time machine and asked what they would change in their life. "They really connected with that aspect," she says. "They really liked discussing their past and how to change the patterns and cycles and work to build a future."

FUTURE WORLD

12

While I was doing research for this book, family friends and art collectors Linda and Leonard Murray suggested that I take a look at the poster art created by MacArthur Fellow Kerry James Marshall for the African Festival of the Arts. The festival is a robust extravaganza held each year in Chicago's Washington Park and is produced by Africa International House. The Murrays work with the festival each year and when they learned I was working in Afrofuturism, they figured that Marshall's commissioned work would be up my cosmic alley. When I asked what the poster depicted, they had a difficult time explaining it, but in short described the work as the "Black Jetsons."

I rushed over to their home to take a look, and the poster was pretty amazing, to say the least. It highlighted a loving family of four living in a space station decked out in African art with a snazzy, to-die-for panoramic view of the Milky Way out their living room window. The kids, a young boy and girl, are seated on a sofa studying Earth via a hologram that hovers over their coffee table. The parents are both in African-accented garb. The father with long dreads playfully wraps his arms around the mother, who is sporting a large head wrap. The family are art collectors as well, and this cozy space pad is decorated with Dogon masks and Yoruba sky art along with a healthy spread of plants. This far-out family moment was one of a kind. Marshall named it *Keeping the Culture.*

After learning about the poster, I was invited by Africa International House president Patrick Saingbey Woodtor and art dealer John A. Martin to discuss Afrofuturism and how *Keeping the Culture* fit into the aesthetic before a group of art collectors.

Afterward, participants, most of whom were unfamiliar with the term, were taken by the futurism and culture in the piece. To my surprise, they were also inspired to share personal stories of their own; true stories of futuristic technologies they'd witnessed long before they hit the market, family stories of time travel, or unique ideas they had on space travel and critical technologies they wanted to invent. Some debated whether the hovering image of Earth was indeed a hologram or a time travel portal. These unassuming crowds of collectors were bound in their Afro-surreal cultural ties to technology and the imagination, a realization triggered by *Keeping the Culture* and having Afrofuturism defined.

Marshall is one of the great artists of our times, and his works are housed in the top collections and museums around the world, including the Smithsonian. At one point, Marshall says his aim was to create as many quality works with black people as possible and to have them posted in the far corners of the world. His success, with his works featured globally, has done just that. But for *Keeping the Culture*, Marshall challenged the conventions about the future. "I just thought it would be interesting to link the idea of the historical past with black people and the diaspora but also look at how that past can be carried along with the people who are evolving toward the future," he says. He purposely combined traditional African art tied to the sky and mysticism along with holograms and space stations, to bridge the idea of an African origin with the transference of culture and family values into a space-friendly future. "It struck me that you rarely see images of black people projecting themselves into the future. When you do, it's almost always the post-apocalyptic type of future where the person is very isolated."

Marshall believes contemplating the future is important. "It comes down to do we really imagine ourselves to be in the future? And if we imagine ourselves into the future, how are we going to be when we get there?" he asks. "Can we be agents of the future or will we be objects of the future, like we were objects of commerce when black folks were brought to the New World?" He's an advocate of the strategic use of the imagination and urges Afrofuturists to ponder how they can have a collective technological advantage that helps shape the world and alleviate disparity. We must be "in front of the developing of the material realities that shape the future," he says. The influencers of the future aren't those who create the next high-profile phone, but rather those who determine whether we'll be using phones in the first place, he adds.

Afrofuturism is a great tool for wielding the imagination for personal change and societal growth. Empowering people to see themselves and their ideas in the future gives rise to innovators and free thinkers, all of whom can pull from the best of the past while navigating the sea of possibilities to create communities, culture, and a new, balanced world. The imagination is the key to progress, and it's the imagination that is all too often smothered in the name of conformity and community standards.

On the one hand, Afrofuturism encourages the beauties of African diasporic cultures and gives people of color a face in the future. But from a global vantage point, the perspective contributes to world knowledge and ideas and includes the perspectives of a group too often deleted from the past and future. Sometimes Afrofuturists address otherness dead-on, while some simply give life to the stories that dance in their mind. But all are aware that the future, technology, and the scope of the imagination have unlimited potential that culture can inform.

Yet the inequities that plagued the past and play out in the present cannot be carried into the future. Afrofuturism provides a prism for examining this issue through art and discourse, but it's a prism that is not exclusive to the diaspora alone. Whether by adopting the aesthetic or the principles, all people can find inspiration or practical use for Afrofuturism to both transform their world and break free of their own set of limitations. The myths of the Dogon or the stories of Samuel Delany can and do enrich lives all over the world. The musical approaches of DJ Spooky or the *Black Kirby* art show provide the cognitive dissonance that many need to rewire their limited view of the world. Good ideas transcend time, space, and culture. To quote the film *V for Vendetta*, ideas are bulletproof.

While teaching yoga to a group of fifth-grade African American girls, for some reason I brought up the rover on Mars. I talked about space tourism and asked how many would be willing to take a ride. All hands shot up. One said she was going to ask her mom to start saving money so they could buy a ticket. Today the tickets are around ninety thousand dollars. But one day, not too far off, the prices will go down, space tourism will be commonplace, and the fact that we lived in a time when it was not will sound like we lived in the age of the dinosaurs when we retell it. Perhaps this young girl, inspired by space travel, will create the latest flying car upgrade. Or maybe, as she's mapping out her Mars trip, she'll write a story about her future, her interstellar travels, and the life force she brings to this red planet neighbor. Perhaps, with a desire to improve the world's conditions, she'll link into a larger group of people in a shared vision of sustainability and equality. Starting with her imagination and implementing ideas through her actions, she'll live the future. The future is ours. Yes, the future is now.

NOTES

Chapter 1: Evolution of a Space Cadet

1. Ingrid LaFleur, "Visual Aesthetics of Afrofuturism," TEDx Fort Greene Salon, *YouTube*, September 25, 2011.

Chapter 2: A Human Fairy Tale Named Black

1. Ytasha Womack, "Dorothy Roberts Debunks Myth of Race," *Post Black Experience*, http://postblackexperience.com/tag/dorothy-roberts/ (Accessed January 10, 2012).
2. Kodwo Eshun, *More Brilliant Than the Sun: Adventures in Sonic Fiction* (UK: Quartet Books, 1998), 175.
3. Saidiya Hartman, *Lose Your Mother* (New York: Farrar, Strauss and Giroux, 2008).
4. Sarah Zielinski, "Henrietta Lacks Immortal Cells," *Smithsonian Magazine*, www.smithsonianmag.com/science-nature/Henrietta-Lacks-Immortal-Cells.html (Accessed January 22, 2010).
5. Ytasha Womack, "Dorothy Roberts Debunks Myth," *Post Black Experience*, http://postblackexperience.com/tag/dorothy-roberts/ (Accessed October 17, 2011).
6. Reynaldo Anderson, "Critical Afrofuturism: A Case Study in Visual Rhetoric, Sequential Art, and Post-Apocalyptic Black Identity" (2012).

Chapter 3: Project Imagination

1. Jeremy Hsu, "Former Astronaut Will Lead 100 Year Starship Effort," *Tech News Daily*, www.technewsdaily.com/5774 -astronaut-lead-100-year-starship.html (Accessed May 21, 2012).
2. Center for Black Studies, "AfroGeeks: Global Blackness and the Digital Sphere," University of California Santa Barbara, www .research.ucsb.edu/cbs/projects/afrogeeks04.html (Accessed March 1, 2012).
3. Mark Dery, "Black to the Future," in *Flame Wars: The Discourse of Cyberculture* (Durham, NC: Duke University Press, 1994), 180.
4. Aaron Smither and Joanna Brenner, "Twitter Use 2012," Pew Internet & American Life Project, http://pewinternet.org/Reports /2012/Twitter-Use-2012/Findings.aspx (Accessed May 31, 2012).

Chapter 4: Mothership in the Key of Mars

1. Amina Khan, "New will.i.am Song Transmitted from Mars Curiosity Rover," *Los Angeles Times*, http://articles.latimes.com /2012/aug/28/science/la-sci-sn-will-i-am-curiosity-mars-rover -track-nasa-20120828 (Accessed August 28, 2012).
2. "Will.i.am NASA Interview at Curiosity Mars Landing 2012," *YouTube*, August 6, 2012.
3. Scott T. Hill, "With Earthbound, CopperWire Creates a Soulful Sci-Fi Space Opera," *Wired*, www.wired.com/underwire/2012/04 /copperwire-earthbound/ (Accessed April 4, 2012).
4. *The Last Angel of History*, directed by John Akomfrah (Icarus Films, 1996).
5. Scot Hacker, "Can You Get to That: The Cosmology of P-Funk," *Stuck Between Stations*, http://stuckbetweenstations.org/2011 /01/11/cosmology-of-pfunk/ (January 11, 2011).
6. Kodwo Eshun, *More Brilliant Than the Sun: Adventures in Sonic Fiction* (UK: Quartet Books, 1998).
7. Eshun, *More Brilliant Than the Sun*.

8. "The Ten Droid Commandments," *HollyGoCrunkly,* http://hollygo
crunkly.tumblr.com/post/746007554/the-ten-droid-commandments
(Accessed May 10, 2012).

Chapter 5: The African Cosmos for Modern Mermaids (Mermen)

1. Malidoma Patrice Somé, *Ritual, Magic, and Inititation in the Life of an African Shaman* (New York: Penguin Group, 1995), 8.
2. Somé, *Ritual, Magic, and Initiation,* 9.
3. Hunter Hindrew and Mamaissii Vivian, "Mami Water Healers Society," *Mami Wata,* www.mamiwata.com/news.html (Accessed June 5, 2012).
4. Aker, "My-stery Images of Mami Wata," *Futuristically Ancient,* http://futuristicallyancient.com/2012/04/18/the-my-stery-images-of-mami-wata (Accessed April 18, 2012).
5. "Last Splash: Azealia Banks Explains the Whole Mermaid Deal," *Spin Magazine,* www.spin.com/articles/last-splash-azealia-banks-explains-whole-mermaid-deal (Accessed July 12, 2012).
6. "African Cosmos," African Institute of Art, http://africa.si.edu/exhibits/cosmos/intro.html (Accessed June 1, 2012).
7. Somé, *Ritual, Magic, and Initiation,* 8–9.

Chapter 6: The Divine Feminine in Space

1. "Martin Luther King Was a Trekkie: Star Trek and Equality," *YouTube* (Accessed January 23, 2011).
2. *Matrix Reloaded,* directed by Lana Wachowski and Andy Wachowski (Warner Brothers, 2003).
3. Gillian Gus Andrews, "Janelle Monae Turns Rhythm and Blues into Science Fiction," *I09,* http://io9.com/5592174/janelle-monae-turns-rhythm-and-blues-into-science-fiction (Accessed July 21, 2010).

4. "Grace Jones," *Elton & Jacobsen*, http://eltonjacobsen.com/2008/06/22/grace-jones (Accessed April 18, 2012).

5. Katerina Wilhelmina, "Grace Jones Quotes," *Chatterbusy Blogspot*, http://chatterbusy.blogspot.com/2012/10/grace-jones-quotes.html (Accessed October 1, 2012).

6. Jennie Ruby, "Women Only Spaces: An Alternative to Patriarchy," *Feminist Reprise*, www.feminist-reprise.org/docs/womonlyspace.htm (Accessed April 22, 2012).

7. Tempestt Hazel, "Black to the Future Series: An Interview with D. Denenge Akpem," *Sixty Inches from Center*, Chicago Arts Archive, http://sixtyinchesfromcenter.org/archive/?p=16638 (Accessed July 23, 2012).

Chapter 7: Pen My Future

1. W. E. B. Du Bois, "The Comet," in *Dark Matter*, edited by Sheree R. Thomas (2000): 5–18.

2. Samuel R. Delany, "Racism and Science Fiction," *New York Review of Science Fiction*, Issue 120, August 1998, www.nyrsf.com/racism-and-science-fiction-.html (Accessed September 1, 2012).

3. Jess Nevins, "The Black Fantastic: Highlights of Pre World War II African and African American Speculative Fiction," *IO9*. http://io9.com/5947122/the-black-fantastic-highlights-of-pre+world-war-ii-african-and-african+american-speculative-fiction (Accessed October 2, 2012).

4. Nevins, "The Black Fantastic."

5. "Afrofuturism, Science Fiction and the History of the Future," *Socialism and Democracy Online*, http://sdonline.org/42/Afrofuturism-science-fiction-and-the-history-of-the-future (Accessed April 20, 2012).

6. "Afrofuturism, Science Fiction," *Socialism and Democracy Online*.

7. Mindy Farabee, "Nalo Hopkinson's Science Fiction and Real Life Family," *Los Angeles Times*, March 21, 2013, http://articles.latimes.com/2013/mar/21/entertainment/la-ca-jc-nalo-hopkinson-20130324.

Chapter 8: Moonwalkers in Paint and Pixels

1. Samantha Burton, "The Africa That I Know," *Bitch*, http://bitchmagazine.org/article/the-africa-that-i-know (Accessed April 15, 2012).
2. Alyx Vesey, "Bechdel Test Canon: Pumzi," *Bitch*, http://bitch magazine.org/post/bechdel-test-canon-pumzi-feminist-film-review (Accessed February 3, 2012).
3. Tempestt Hazel, "Black to the Future Series. An Interview with Cauleen Smith," *Sixty Inches from Center*, Chicago Arts Archive, http://sixtyinchesfromcenter.org/archive/?p=17269 (Accessed September 4, 2012).
4. Lupe Fiasco, "Lupe Fiasco: This City Is a Robot," *Chicago Sun-Times*, www.suntimes.com/lifestyles/splash/12870919-418/lupe-fiasco-this-city-is-a-robot.html (Accessed June 5, 2012).
5. "The Mysterious Phenomenon That Transforms Average Songwriters Into Legends," *Songwriting Secrets*, www.songwriting-secrets.net/songwriting-inspiration.html (Accessed June 1, 2012).

Chapter 9: A Clock for Time Travelers

1. Fred Alan Wolf, *Fred Alan Wolf*, www.fredalanwolf.com (Accessed April 10, 2012).
2. Duffy Damien and John Jennings, *Black Comix* (New York: Mark Batty Publishing, 2010), 164.
3. Wolf, www.fredalanwolf.com (Accessed April 10, 2012).
4. Jo Walton, "Time Travel and Slavery," *Tor*, www.tor.com/blogs/2009/04/octavia-butlers-kindred (Accessed June 1, 2012).

INDEX

Index

Index

Index

ABOUT THE AUTHOR

Ytasha L. Womack is a filmmaker, futurist, and the author of *Post Black: How a New Generation Is Redefining African American Identity* and *2212: Book of Rayla*. She is the creator of the Rayla 2212 sci-fi multimedia series, the director of the award-winning film *The Engagement*, the producer and writer of *Love Shorts*, and the coeditor of *Beats Rhymes and Life: What We Love and Hate About Hip Hop*. She has written for many publications including *Ebony* and the *Chicago Tribune* and has appeared on *E! True Hollywood Stories: Rappers Wives*.